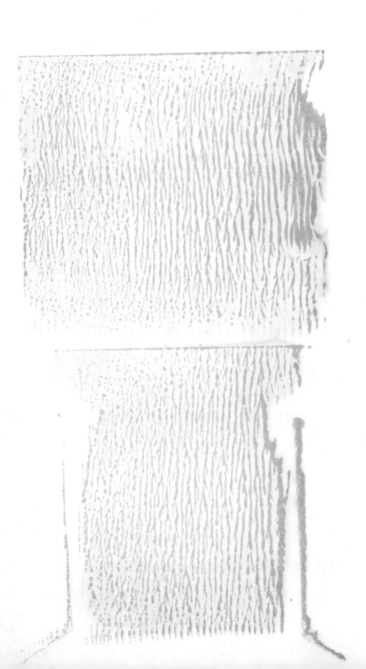

Black Women Composers:

A Genesis

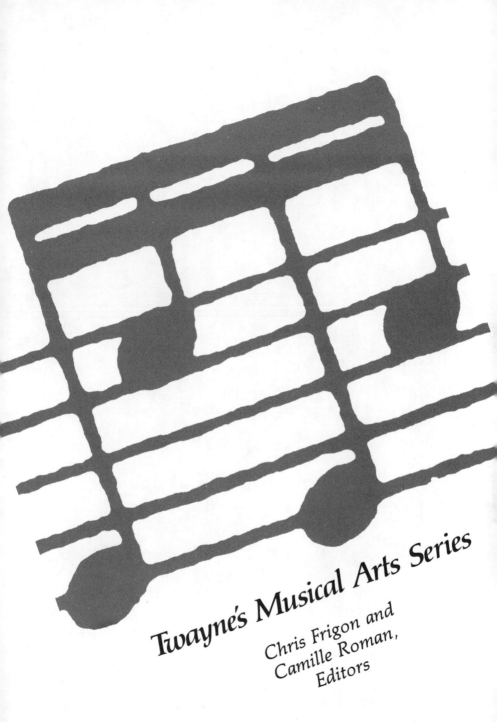

Twayne's Musical Arts Series

Chris Frigon and
Camille Roman,
Editors

Black Women Composers:

A Genesis

Mildred Denby Green

Twayne Publishers

Published in 1983 by Twayne Publishers,
A Division of G. K. Hall & Co.
70 Lincoln Street, Boston, Mass. 02111

Printed on permanent/durable
acid-free paper and bound in
the United States of America

First Printing

Book design by Barbara Anderson

Library of Congress Cataloging in Publication Data
Green, Mildred Denby.
Black women composers.

(Twayne's music series)
Bibliography: p. 145
Includes index.
1. Afro-American women composers—Biography.
I. Title. II. Series.
ML390.G83   780'.92'2   [B]   81-198
ISBN 0-8057-9450-6   AACR2

Contents

About the Author

Mildred Denby Green is an associate professor of music at LeMoyne-Owen College, Memphis, Tennessee. She holds a bachelor of science degree with a major in music education from Ohio State University and master of music education and doctor of music education degrees from the University of Oklahoma, Norman. The LeMoyne-Owen College Choir, under her leadership, performs works by black women composers. She has published Part I of her article "Women of Vision: Black Women Composers" in *Black Pearl*. She also lectures and conducts workshops on music of the black church.

Preface

We know very little about the black American women composers of the twentieth century who blend jazz, blues, and spiritual
elements and the traditions of Western European music. I have
therefore written *Black Women Composers*. In this introductory
study, we will examine the works of Florence Price, Margaret
Bonds, Julia Perry, Evelyn Pittman, and Lena McLin.

Sources are sparse. This is not surprising; it merely attests to our
neglect of both black classical musicians and female musicians.
However, two references were especially helpful for their discus-
sions of Afro-American music: *The Music of Black Americans: A
History* by Eileen Southern and *Black American Music: Past and
Present* by Hildred Roach. *The Negro in Music and Art*, compiled
and edited by Lindsay Patterson, offered "A Reminiscence" by
Margaret Bonds. "Black Composers and Their Piano Music," from
The American Music Teacher, the periodical of the Music Teachers
National Association, provided valuable information on Florence
Price and Margaret Bonds. Finally, I must mention two publications
by Dominique-Rene de Lerma, founder and former director of The
Black Music Center at Indiana University: *Black Music in Our
Culture* and *Reflections on Afro-American Music*. Lena McLin's
article "Black Music in Church and School" appeared in *Black
Music in Our Culture*.

To select the composers, I examined lists of black women composers supplied by the Black Music Center at Indiana University
and the Library of Congress. Since the catalog made no distinction
between composers of serious and popular music, I surveyed biographical dictionaries, books, and articles on black musicians to
identify the composers of serious music. In addition, I consulted
several prominent musicians for names of black women composers
whom they knew either personally or through their music. These
persons were: the late Spencer Norton, research professor emeritus,

School of Music, the University of Oklahoma; Carol Brice Carey, professor of voice, School of Music, the University of Oklahoma; Eileen Southern, professor of music and of Afro-American Studies (chairman), Harvard University; publisher/editor of *The Black Perspective in Music*; author; T. J. Anderson, composer, chairman of music, Tufts University, Medford, Massachusetts; Colonius Davis, professor of music, Southhampton College, Long Island, New York.

My study of vocal music and work with choral groups naturally led me to consider those composers whose works I had either performed with choirs or had heard in concert. Research revealed more black women composers than a study of this nature could encompass so I have limited my work to the following five. Florence Price was the first black woman to receive international recognition as a composer. A graduate of the New England Conservatory of Music in Boston, she represents the first generation of black American women composers. Her contemporaries were the black male composers R. Nathaniel Dett, Hall Johnson, William Grant Still, and William Dawson.

Margaret Bonds, a student of Florence Price, represents the second generation of black women composers. She studied with William Dawson and received her bachelor's and master's degrees from Northwestern University. Her association with many of the well-known black poets, artists, and musicians left a decided mark on her music. Black male composers of her era include Howard Swanson and Ulysses Kay.

Julia Perry wrote in an eclectic style which established her international reputation. She received her bachelor's and master's degrees from Westminster Choir College and studied composition with Luigi Dallapiccola in Italy and Nadia Boulanger in France.

Evelyn Pittman is both a music educator and composer. She studied composition with Harrison Kerr at the University of Oklahoma, where she received a master's degree, and with Nadia Boulanger in France.

Lena McLin, another music educator and composer, studied composition with Leonora Brown and Willis Lawrence James at Spelman College in Atlanta and with Stella Roberts at the American

Conservatory of Music in Chicago. She also studied electronic music at Roosevelt University in Chicago.

I obtained selected scores from several sources, including publishers and the private collections of Carol Brice Carey, Neumon Leighton, Evelyn Pittman, Ruby Clark, Nelmatilda Ritchie Woodard, and Lawrence and Djane Richardson.

I have analyzed only published compositions which represent the composers' styles. I included compositions in the various media found among the published works of each composer unless the work was out of print or otherwise unavailable.

When I began this study in 1972, four of the five composers were still living. Margaret Bonds died in the spring of 1972, and Julia Perry died in 1979. I conducted personal interviews with the composer when possible and obtained biographical information in interviews with former teachers, friends, and relatives. Other sources included letters from the composers, their relatives, and friends; articles; reviews of works and concerts; unpublished materials; and reference books.

I am indebted to Camille Roman and Chris Frigon, editors of Twayne's Musical Arts Series, for their encouragement, advice, and valuable criticism. I owe special thanks to Dr. Ernest L. Trumble, professor of music at the Oklahoma University School of Music, for his invaluable aid in gathering material on the role of women in European music, and for his encouragement.

I am especially grateful to Evelyn Pittman, Lena McLin, and the late Julia Perry, who responded to requests for interviews, biographical information, and other materials; to the late Ruby Clark of Chicago and the late Neumon Leighton of Memphis, Tennessee, both of whom provided information and arranged interviews with relatives and friends of Florence Price and Margaret Bonds; to James C. McKeever, director of development and alumni affairs at Westminster Choir College; to John Peck, director of archives, Talbott Library, Westminster Choir College; and to Mrs. Jean E. Harris, media consultant, State Library, New Jersey Department of Education, for providing material on Julia Perry. I express sincere appreciation to Mrs. Samiephyne M. Ross for her generous advice and for typing the final manuscript.

Acknowledgment is due Carl Fischer, Inc., G. Schirmer, Inc., Galaxy Music Corporation, Theodore Presser Company, Handy Brothers Music Co., Inc., Peer-Southern Organization, General Words and Music Co., Publishers, and Evelyn Pittman for permission to include reproductions of the musical examples used in this study.

Finally, I wish to express my deep gratitude to my family: Reuben I, Reuben II, Howard, my mother (Wanetah B. Davis) and stepfather Waldo. Without their help, understanding, love, and devotion, this project would have been impossible. To them and to the memory of my father, this work is affectionately dedicated.

Chronology

1888   Florence B. Price born in Little Rock, Arkansas, April 9.

1907   Graduates with honors from the New England Conservatory of Music, Boston; begins teaching in Cotton Plant, Arkansas.

1908– Teaches at Clark College, Atlanta, Georgia, and then at
1912   Shorter College in North Little Rock, Arkansas.

1910   Evelyn Pittman born in McAlester, Oklahoma, January 6.

1913   Margaret Bonds born in Chicago, Illinois, March 3.

1924   Julia Perry born in Lexington, Kentucky, March 25.

1927   Price moves to Chicago with husband and family.

1929   Lena McLin born in Atlanta, Georgia, September 5.

1932   Price and Bonds receive Wanamaker Awards in Composition.

1933   Bonds receives bachelor's degree from Northwestern University, Evanston, Illinois.
Pittman receives bachelor's degree from Spelman College, Atlanta, Georgia.
Symphony in E minor by Price premiered by Chicago Symphony Orchestra at World's Fair in Chicago.

1934   Bonds receives master's degree from Northwestern University; performs *Piano Concerto in F minor* by Price with Chicago Women's Symphony Orchestra in Chicago.

1937   *My Soul's Been Anchored in de Lord* published by Price.

1938   Evelyn Pittman Choir organized in Oklahoma City; represents Oklahoma and Texas at Chicago World's Fair.

1939   Bonds moves to New York City.

1941   *Songs to a Dark Virgin* by Price published.

1942   *The Negro Speaks of Rivers* by Bonds published.

1944   *Rich Heritage* (book of stories and songs about famous blacks) by Pittman published; revised in 1968.

1947	Perry receives bachelor's degree from Westminster Choir College, Princeton, New Jersey.
1948	Perry receives master's degree from Westminster.
	Pittman studies at Juilliard.
1949	*Two Traditional Spirituals* by Price published.
	Sit Down Servant by Pittman published.
	Perry studies at Tanglewood.
1950	Perry studies at Juilliard.
	Ruth (a cantata) by Perry performed April 16 at Riverside Church in New York City; Perry is assistant coach and participant in Columbia Opera Workshop.
1951	McLin receives bachelor's degree from Spelman College, Atlanta, Georgia.
	Perry studies with Dallapiccola at Tanglewood.
1952	Perry travels on a Guggenheim Fellowship to Europe to study with Dallapiccola in Italy and Boulanger in France; receives Fountainbleau Award.
	Bonds gives Town Hall debut as pianist in New York.
	Rocka Mah Soul by Pittman published.
1953	Price dies in Chicago, June 3.
1954	Original (shorter) version of *The Ballad of the Brown King* by Bonds premiered on December 12, New York City.
	Pittman receives master's degree from the University of Oklahoma; completes *Cousin Esther* (opera).
	Stabat Mater for contralto and string orchestra by Perry published.
1955	Perry makes second trip to Europe on a Guggenheim to study with Dallapiccola.
1956	Pittman goes to Paris to study with Boulanger; *Cousin Esther* (excerpts) performed in Paris, France.
	Perry studies conducting with Adone Zecchi and Alceo Galliera in Italy (summers, 1956-58).
1957	Perry organizes and conducts concerts in Europe for United States Information Agency.
	Cousin Esther by Pittman performed several times in Paris.
1958	Pittman begins teaching in Woodlands High School, Hartsdale, New York.
1959	*Three Dream Portraits* by Bonds published.

1960	*The Ballad of the Brown King* (revised and lengthened) by Bonds televised on "Christmas U.S.A.," December 11, CBS.
1961	*The Ballad of the Brown King* published.
1962	*Cousin Esther* (excerpts) by Pittman premiered in New York City at Carnegie Hall.
1964	Bonds receives ASCAP Awards (1964-66).
	Perry wins American Academy and National Institute of Arts and Letters Award.
1965	Bonds studies composition with Robert Starer at Juilliard.
1966	*Homunculus C. F.* (for percussion, harp, and piano) by Perry published.
1967	Perry teaches at Florida A. & M. University in Tallahassee.
	Bonds receives alumni medal from Northwestern University.
1968	Leontyne Price commissions Bonds to arrange a group of spirituals; Bonds goes to California.
1969	Perry serves as visiting music consultant at the Atlanta Colleges Center; receives honorable mention in ASCAP Awards to Women Composers for symphonic and concert music.
	McLin becomes head of music department, Kenwood High School, Chicago.
1970	*Freedom Child* (excerpts) by Pittman premiered in New York City.
	McLin named leading black choral composer by National Association of Negro Musicians (NANM).
1971	*Freedom Child* by Pittman completed and performed in New York and several Southern states including Atlanta, Georgia, before the Martin Luther King family.
	McLin named outstanding composer by Critics Association.
1972	Bonds dies in Los Angeles, April 26; her *Credo* (for chorus and orchestra) is premiered by Los Angeles Symphony Orchestra conducted by Zubin Mehta.
	Freedom Child by Pittman performed on European tour.
	McLin named "Best Teacher of the Year," Chicago.
1973	McLin's *Let the People Sing Praise Unto the Lord; Free At*

Last (cantata) published; McLin receives Virginia Union University Award for Outstanding Composer.

1975 McLin receives honorary degree (L.H.D.) from Virginia Union University, Richmond, Virginia.

1976 Pittman retires from her teaching position in New York and moves back to Oklahoma City.

1977 *Pulse—A Music History* by McLin published.
The Oklahoma Historical Society presents excerpts from *Jim Noble* (docu-music drama) by Pittman in Oklahoma City.

1978 *Freedom Child* by Pittman performed during tour of England and Scotland.

1979 Perry dies in Akron, Ohio, April 29.

Chapter One

Women in Music

In 1936 black musician Shirley Graham surveyed black American music from the time of the Fisk Jubilee Singers to 1935 when America heard William Dawson's *Negro Folk Symphony* played by the Philadelphia Orchestra on an NBC radio broadcast. She observed: "Spirituals to symphonies in less than fifty years! How could they attempt it? Among her millions of citizens, America can boast of but a few symphonists. . . . And one of these symphonists is a woman! Florence B. Price." [1]

The history of women composers properly begins in prehistoric times. Cro-Magnon man, from the Upper Paleolithic Age which ended before 10,000 B.C., danced to probably the earliest-known music in his hunting and fertility rites. Of course, there is no direct evidence of the music itself, but pictures of dancers in caves of southwestern France and northern Spain suggest a musical accompaniment possibly like that of indigenous people living today in Australia and South Africa. [2] The paintings of the dancing sorcerers and magicians depict males in grotesque animal masks. [3] Likenesses of woman in the small, isolated statues and engravings show her as childbearer with greatly enlarged breasts, hips, and thighs. In this patriarchal society women probably could not even watch the magical male rites. [4]

Artistic scenes from possibly 10,000 to 3,000 B.C. show women dancing for the first time. In one famous painting in Cogul, Spain, female dancers sway in bell-shaped skirts, while being circled by a nude male satyr. [5] Judging from the artwork, one can imagine a softer and more graceful dancing music than the music of the earlier male dances.

15

In dances of around 1,500 B.C., men leapt and women stepped; men strove outward and upward and women tended to inward, closed forms; men made large movements and women made small ones. The melodies of the women were symmetrical and simple with regular rhythm as opposed to the more rhapsodic, undisciplined music of the men.[6] The men did most of the singing and performed the war, hunting, and sun dances as well as the animal spirit and male initiation dances; women concerned themselves with fertility dances and the events of rain, harvest, birth, and the consecration of girls and female shamans.

With the development of literacy European and African civilizations began to emerge. Black American women share the heritage of both areas; we will examine each one separately.

I Women in European Music

In contrast with most of the ancient peoples who followed the patterns of the patriarchal societies where men hunted and fought and women farmed and cared for children, the Cretans developed a relatively egalitarian society for both women and men. In the pre-Mycenaean, Mycenaean, and Minoan cultures, women did not wear veils or remain secluded. They served as priestesses to the most important Cretan deity, Earth Mother. The Minoans apparently pursued a matrilineal and matriarchal structure, not unusual among the pre-Aryan groups of the Mediterranean. Cretan art showed "female" influences: imagination, freedom, and exuberance.[7]

The "free and open" society of the Cretans lived in classical Greece only in the tragedies of Aeschylus, Sophocles, and Euripides, reflecting the influence of Homer. The comedies of Aristophanes, however, placed women in a much more realistic, restricted setting. In the Athens of the fifth century, women lived in very strict seclusion, forbidden to leave home except for funerals, weddings, and religious ceremonies. The only men they could talk to were relatives and slaves. Since most of the scenes in the comedies took place in the open air, respectable women did not appear frequently as characters in the comedies. The male chorus, *cho-*

rautae, sometimes represented women. In Aristophanes' play *Frogs*, the clouds portrayed women and the chorus of initiates included both men and women. This theatrical transvestism reached extremes in Aristophanes' *Women in Council* where the *chorautae* are men dressed to represent women who are trying to disguise themselves as men. All this emphasizes the absence of Greek women in the performance of the music of the great Athenian tragedies and comedies.

Greece does offer us, however, the work of Sappho, one of its great poets, who expressed her inner feelings with a delicacy and beauty of language seldom equalled. Sappho's poetry and music required memorization or improvisation in the proper mode, observing the rhythm of the words. The stanzaic rhythms exhibited less repetition and more diversity than our modern strophic structures. The melody of the poem followed the pitch-accented Greek language and the mode to which it belonged. According to Aristoxenus' *Harmonics*, Sappho invented the Mixolydian mode.

Greek women could perform in festivals considered traditional for them. They sang the *Paean*, for example, a customary hymn accompanying public ritual sacrifices at Delphi, except those offered during the three-month winter absences of Apollo. In "Hymn to the Delian Apollo," Delian maidens sang what is apparently a standing hymn to Artemis and Apollo. It is essentially a *partheneion* or maiden-song, a processional song-dance allied to the hymn, but still containing secular elements.

The famous performers on instruments were all male, such as Terpander, known for his *nomoi kitharodikoi* (vocal solos accompanied by lyre). Women performed professionally on the aulos or oboe as we learn from the lyric poet Mimnermus of Smyrna, believed the first to make the elegy the vehicle for mournful, erotic strains. Performers probably recited these elegies rhythmically to the accompaniment of the aulos.

A Middle ages

St. Paul sums up the attitude of early Christians toward women in the first epistle to Timothy (2:11–12): "Let the woman learn in silence with all subjection. But I suffer not a woman to teach, nor to usurp authority over the man, but to be in silence." Among other restrictions, this meant that she must not make music, especially religious music.

This philosophy concerning women, which so profoundly influenced Christianity, reflected the ultra-conservative Yemenite Jewish prejudices toward women. In the congregations of Paul's time, men and children, but not women, joined in the congregational songs. The women had their own music. They accompanied themselves on frame drums or cymbals which they beat with their hands during the melody.[8]

The women in the early and medieval Christian church also developed their own music. In the monastic establishments, they could sing in the ritual of the Divine Office but not in the Mass.[9] Their activities contributed greatly to the cultural climate that produced Hildegard of Bingen (1098–1179), a mystic, prophet, councillor, and correspondent of the pope, the emperor, and princes. Besides creating music and religious poetry, she wrote on theology, natural science, and medicine. Of noble birth, she had an excellent education.

Her musical works are the first of their kind. We still possess a morality play with music, *Ordo virtutum*, 35 antiphons, 18 responsories, 6 sequences, 10 hymns, and miscellaneous pieces including a Kyrie.[10] The works are in the style of simple plainchant melodies. No real difference exists between the style of the *Ordo virtutum* and the hymns. Beside the traditional repertoire of plainchants, the work of countless anonymous individuals over several centuries, Hildegard's chants seem repetitive and limited in melodic vocabulary. Possibly she simply improvised them for a scribe to take down in musical notation. These works are stronger as poetry than as music; their importance lies more in their mere existence than in any profound musical value.[11]

B   The Renaissance

As polyphonic music developed from the twelfth century forward to the Renaissance, musical textures became thicker and musical notation became very complicated, especially in the Ars Nova. One literally could not write in the polyphonic idiom without considerable training in subjects such as counterpoint and modal theory. No evidence exists that women studied these subjects; no polyphony by women of this time survives. Daughters of noblemen learned polyphonic music to sing ayres, ditties, and madrigals and to play the virginal or harpsichord. Several noblewomen developed a special interest in music. Isabella d'Este, for example, supported the flourishing school of Frottolists in Mantua at the turn of the sixteenth century. Margaret of Austria, regent of the Netherlands (1480-1530), associated with the composer Pierre de la Rue.

Mary, Queen of Scots (1542-1587), was one of the few noble or royal women who also composed. Born in Scotland of a French mother and Scottish father, she followed the longstanding compositional tradition of British monarchs. Mary wrote many songs; two attained popularity in her lifetime. The average woman, however, could only nurture the arts; she could not pursue them as professions.

A few women of the late Renaissance and early Baroque were accomplished performers. Some of them took the next logical step— composition. They published collections of madrigals or motets, principally in Italy. Many were nuns; some, abbesses of their cloisters. Others were daughters of composers. A few were simply Renaissance musicians who happened to be women.

Among the first women to receive widespread recognition as a performer-composer was Maddelana Mezari. Born around 1540 in Vicenza, she studied voice and lute and achieved fame as a lutanist. She successfully taught composition to the poet Antonio Molino in his later years, and in gratitude he dedicated to her his collection of *Dilettevoli Madrigali* for four voices (1586). She published her first book of twenty-five madrigals for four voices in Venice (Scotto) in 1568 and the second collection of twenty-one madrigals two years later. Thirteen years later, she published her first book of twenty-one madrigals for five voices. Several of her madrigals appeared in other Venetian publications as well. Musicologists have transcribed and studied so few of these works that their merits are unknown.[12]

Two sisters, Raffaella and Vittoria Aleotti of Ferrara, achieved widespread fame through the Catholic Church.[13] Born around 1570, Raffaella entered the Augustinian cloister of San Vito in Ferrara where fine musical performance was a tradition. She enthusiastically played the organ and, in 1593, became director of vocal and instrumental ensembles; later, she became prioress of the cloister. The refinement of the performances during her tenure drew praise from writers and composers. Under her direction the nuns of San Vito gave concerts for Pope Clement VIII and one in honor of Margaret of Austria, consort of Philip III, King of Spain. She was also acclaimed as a composer of madrigals and motets. Vittoria, on the other hand, published only madrigals—a book entitled *Ghirlanda dei Madrigali a 4 voci* (Venice, 1593). In addition, the Ferrarese madrigal group commissioned a madrigal from her which they published in their collection *Il Giardino de' musici Ferraresi* published by Vincenti in Venice in 1591. As was frequently the case with women throughout history, she found her name in the madrigal collection printed in its masculine form "Vittorio," either by accident or design. In the nineteenth century, women composers often deliberately used masculine names to escape prejudice.

C The Baroque

The creation of opera in Italy toward the end of the sixteenth century was one of the most important events in the history of women in music. It influenced musical style in almost every genre, as well as techniques of singing, and patterns of patronage. It also liberated the woman musician, eventually making her the equal or superior of the male in status, in performance at least.

By the time opera developed, professional companies of actors and actresses—the *commedia dell'arte*—were already well established. Because women performed rather freely in theatrical roles in Italy, they soon made their mark in opera in spite of prejudice.[14]

In Florence, Francesca Caccini (1581 or 1588-c. 1640) the daughter of Giulio Caccini (one of the original composers in the Camerata), and her sister not only achieved fame in opera as performers, but also composed music for opera and ballet. Francesca published songs for one and two voices, and two ballets, as well as music for masquerades, intermezzi, and operas by other composers. She also wrote an unpublished opera.[15]

Barbara Strozzi, the adoptive daughter of the Venetian librettist Guilio Strozzi, became known as a singer and composer of arias in 1636 while she was still in her teens.[16]

In sacred music, one of the most renowned composers was the nun Catterina Assandra. Her reputation extended beyond Italy, as evidenced by the inclusion of two of her motets in a collection entitled *Siren coelestis* published in Munich in 1616 by A. Berg, and in another entitled *Promptuarium musicum* published in Strassburg in 1622 by P. Ledertz.[17]

The music of most of the women composers of this era needs transcription and study in context with the other music of the period. Until this occurs, we will not be able to evaluate their contributions.

D   The Enlightenment

Throughout the eighteenth century, women grew in prominence as composers, performers, and patrons of music. This does not imply, however, that women became equals or competitors with men. The number of women who composed was far smaller than the number of men, as one would expect, because composition and performance of music remained one of the honorable professions only for men.

Women, however, made great strides. Francesca Caccini wrote and produced the first opera by a woman. Barbara Strozzi had her opera produced in Venice in 1659. No other opera by a woman appeared until near the end of the seventeenth century when Elizabeth Claude de la Guerre (1669-1729) of Paris wrote an opera produced at the Royal Academy on March 15, 1694.[18]

In the eighteenth century, eight women wrote twenty-one operas which received performances. For example, Parisienne Julie Candeille wrote a comic opera during the French Revolution which had 154 successive performances following its premiere and remained in the *Comédie Française* repertoire for thirty-five years. She also succeeded in having it translated into several different languages and published.[19]

In Italy, Maria Teresa Agnesi composed seven operas in Milan between 1747 and 1771 that received performances in Milan, Naples, and Venice. Her reputation as a composer prompted an invitation to visit Mozart in the Cloister San Marco in Milan on his first Italian trip.[20]

In Germany, all the women composers of opera were of aristocratic birth. Since the aristocracy provided their daughters with a musical education, many tried composing. However, a few, such as Anna Amalie, princess of Prussia (sister of Frederick the Great); Maria Antonia Walpurgis, grand duchess of Saxony; Amalia Anna, duchess of Saxe-Weimar; and Maria Theresa, countess of Ahlefeldt, composed works above the dilettante level.

Anna Amalie (1723-1787) took her first music lessons from her brother Frederick. Later she wrote a cantata *Der Tod Jesu*, which pre-dates Johann Gottlieb Graun's work on the same subject. She also wrote several instrumental movements, a trio for organ, and other choral works.[21]

Later, Maria Paulowna, grand duchess of Weimar and daughter of Tsar Paul I of Russia, studied with Liszt and composed piano music. Liszt used one of her themes for the fourth of his set of *Consolations*.

E Nineteenth century

In the late eighteenth and early nineteenth centuries, European women composers wrote in much larger quantity than before. Most of the work remains unpublished, however. Women found resistance from the public, male composers, and critics.

During this century, countries on the periphery of Germany, Austria, Italy, and France began to produce both male and female composers and performers of note. Some of the more important came from Poland, Norway, England, and, later, from North and South America.

Nineteenth century women taught and established their own schools and wrote treatises on their teaching methods and philosophies. Many women composers of this period came from families in which the father, brother, or husband was a professional musician. The most famous of these is Clara Schumann (1819-1896), pianist-composer-teacher and the wife of Robert Schumann. She achieved her greatest success as a pianist, but she also taught, composed, and arranged, as well as editing her husband's works and letters. While she did not highly value her own compositions, her husband did.

He published three of her songs as numbers 2, 4, and 11 of his Op. 37, twelve songs on texts from Rückert's *Liebesfrühling*. He wrote an essay on her work *Soirée for Piano*, Op. 6, for her eighteenth birthday. Frédéric Chopin also praised Clara Schumann's compositional talents.

After her marriage in 1840 a change of style appeared in her works, especially in the songs. She wrote, for example, three preludes and fugues (Op. 16) and a piano trio, Op. 17, probably her finest work. In the trio she combines the facile melodic writing of Felix Mendelssohn with the firm and often unexpected harmonic structure of her husband's music. After her husband's death in 1856, she composed little more.

While Clara Schumann found a devoted promoter in her father, Fanny Mendelssohn, Felix's sister, met rejection from her father, Abraham Mendelssohn. He had an aversion to seeing his daughter play the piano in public. He admonished her on her twenty-third birthday, "you must become more steady and collected, and prepare more earnestly and soberly for your real calling, the only calling of a young woman—I mean the state of a housewife."[22] Accepting her father's decision, she married, and directed her talents to promoting her brother's career. She did not appear in public as a pianist until she was thirty-three years old. Then she played Felix's g minor piano concerto at a charity concert with the full support of her husband. Felix opposed the publication of any of her music under her own name to spare her adverse criticism.[23] When she did publish two books of her songs, Felix performed one of his favorites at a recital in Leipzig, and wrote to his sister that there "was much applause after it was over. . . . I thank you in the name of the public of Leipzig and elsewhere for publishing it against my wish." After her death in 1847, her *Piano Trio in D Major*, Op. 11, was published. Unfortunately, none of this music is in print today.

The nineteenth century also witnessed the emergence of the first American women composers to receive acclaim. The South American composer Teresa Carreño (1853-1917) from Venezuela was a piano virtuoso. She studied with Louis Gottschalk and G. A. Matthias in Paris and with Anton Rubinstein in New York.[24] She toured the world, and, with the Bavarian pianist Sophie Mentor, ranked as one of the greatest pianists of her time. She composed many virtuoso pieces, etudes, waltzes, a string quartet, and the Venezuelan national hymn.

The first North American woman to achieve recognition was Amy Marcy Cheney (1867-1944), better known as Mrs. H. H. A. Beach.[25] A child prodigy from the United States, she made her debut as a concert pianist in Boston at age sixteen. A year later, she played the Chopin *Concerto in f Minor* with the Boston Symphony Orchestra and performed the Mendelssohn *Piano Concerto in g Minor* with Theodore Thomas conducting the orchestra.[26] She toured Europe as a pianist and heard her works performed by major European orchestras. Her "Gaelic" symphony especially delighted the Germans. When she returned to the United States, she devoted herself completely to composition and found much support. The Chicago World's Fair commissioned *Festival Jubilate*, the Trans-Mississippi Fair at Omaha, Nebraska, commissioned *Song of Welcome* in 1898, and a Panama-Pacific Exhibition in San Francisco commissioned *Panama Hymn* in 1915. She wrote over eighty works—choral, symphonic, and chamber music, concertos, and sonatas—in every idiom except theater music. She is associated with the New England school of composers which included George Whitfield Chadwick, Arthur Foote, and Horatio Parker.

F   The twentieth century

Women composers, teachers, performers, and writers on music are more prevalent today than during any other period in their musical history. For the purposes of this book, we will close our brief survey of European women composers with a glimpse of the renowned French composition teacher, Nadia Boulanger.

Boulanger came from a long line of musicians. Her grandmother, Marie-Julie Boulanger, pursued a successful career as a mezzo-soprano in the Paris Opéra.[27] Her father, Ernest-Henri-Alexandre, taught composition and voice at the Paris Conservatory.

Both Nadia and her sister Lilli composed early in life. Nadia, however, abandoned composition to devote herself fully to her teaching, which was distinguished by a strict technique, and a comprehensive organization and exploration of styles. She influenced three of the black women composers in this study: Margaret Bonds, Evelyn Pittman, and Julia Perry.

II Women in African Music

In contrast to the history of women musicians of Europe, the history of African women musicians is sparsely documented. We also have few studies of the music itself.

We know today that Africa is not culturally homogeneous. The northern region of Africa has a kinship with Middle Eastern cultures and languages; the southern, with European languages and culture brought by traders, missionaries, and colonists. Therefore, one finds diversity in the music.

African music has two general characteristics: percussive sounds and polyphony (two or more tones sounded together) made up of parallel intervals, complex rhythms, and ostinatos, often used in combination to create more complex polyrhythms. Vocal music is prominent since it provides verbal communication and allows group participation in music. Since many African languages are tonal and the melodies tend to follow speech intonation and rhythms, many instrumental melodies are simply instrumental versions of vocal melodies or sequences of melodic patterns. The scales in both the vocal and instrumental music derive from four to seven step tunings. These tunings may be equidistant, that is, having equal intervals between tones, or nonequidistant. The selection of scale steps and actual pitches varies from one community to another.

Even with the division of Africa in the nineteenth and twentieth centuries, one group has kept intact its distinctive female-dominated culture which predates Islamic or Middle Eastern conquests: the Muslim Berber people called the Tuareg, who live as nomads in the western portion of the Sahara Desert.[28] The ancestry of a family is traced matrilineally. Women guard the intellectual and artistic activities and receive education. Men, rather than women, wear veils and remain illiterate. In fact, Tuareg women have achieved fame as poets and musicians in Africa.

The creation of music in traditional African societies usually takes place at a social event where a group assembles for recreation or ceremonies. Although public group musical activities are the most common, they do not exclude individual performances by a child, man, or woman. When a child loses his first tooth, for example, he sings a special song to celebrate. Individual adults perform music for their own pleasure or for children, or for both. A mother may sing a cradle song which entertains her child but which also contains certain expressions of a more mature level. Domestic songs sung alone or in a group accompany grinding meal, pounding wood, or making a new floor.[29]

Many African societies recognize a wide variety of songs and group them into sets, categories of music named for an activity, event, performer, or the function it performs.[30] An example among the Akan of Ghana is the group of songs called *asrayere* (visiting wives) performed by women when the men are at war, since the women assemble to wish their men well through songs. These same songs become *mmobomme* (songs of prayer) when sung to wish an individual well.[31]

Women create and perform lullabies and songs at puberty rites, births, and funerals. In some parts of Africa, secret societies for women control the puberty rites for girls. In Sierra Leone, the Bandu is a powerful society that regards the music of this puberty rite as one of the "secrets of life" to be passed from one generation to the next.[32]

In several societies, puberty ceremonies are elaborate. The Adangme women of Ghana perform the *dipo* puberty ceremonies. The girls receive several weeks of intensive lessons on motherhood, the special music and dancing of the rite, and the customs and history of their society. At the end of the training period, they hold musical processions, feasts, and singing and dancing parties.[33]

Women in the eastern, central and southern regions perform rites for healing and correcting mental disorders, singing and accompanying themselves with drums and rattles.[34] At certain funerals they wail in choral laments or sing dirges individually. Dirges exist for lineages and clans, as well as specified individuals. Among the Akan of Ghana, it is the social duty of women to mourn their relatives with special dirges, so many mothers teach their daughters these songs, especially those for mourning their parents.[35]

African societies stress exposure to music rather than formal instruction. The mother introduces the child to the music of the culture by rocking him or her to music or singing nonsense syllables that imitate drum rhythms.[36] Mothers also carry their children on their backs to public ceremonies and rituals, exposing them to the music and dances performed by adults.

Restrictions exist pertaining to the playing of musical instruments; they are usually based on age and sex. Often women do not play drums. In some instances they may play only one type of drum: the Akan permit women to play only the hourglass drums.[37] In Tanzania, the Wagogo restrict drumming to performances by women since the men usually sing with gong-like idiophones when they require percussion accompaniment.[38] In southern and eastern Africa women play drums at special ceremonials. In several areas only the women play such instruments as rattles and gourd tubes.

In northeastern Ghana, adults send little girls playing rod rattles into rice fields to scare away birds. Young girls and unmarried women of this area also play rattles to attract attention in the market places.[39]

In several African communities, women dominate as musicmakers. They create music for marriages, funerals, prayers, lullabies, work, war, travel, and greeting visitors. Foreordained women become poet-musicians and are usually respected composers of songs paid handsomely by the chiefs to serve as official songsters and leaders of other women in chorus. These predestined women receive encouragement from early childhood to cultivate their musical talents.

III Black American Women in Music

Both male and female black Americans carried forward the African heritage. In spontaneous group experiences, they improvised spirituals, work songs, hollers, and dance songs. As in Africa, folklore passed from generation to generation unwritten and anonymous. Using European musical practices, American blacks learned the notation of music and preserved what had been previously improvised; composers could now be identified.

Black women slaves in colonial America kept the African traditions alive through their story telling and singing. Two of these women achieved recognition for their abilities in this art: Lucy Terry, also known as Luce Bijah, of Deerfield, Rhode Island, and Senegambia of Narragansett, Rhode Island. Many other black women slaves also entertained audiences with their tales and songs of Africa.[40]

In the bleak years of slavery, women assumed musical prominence as the Christian church assumed a central place in the lives of black people. During the eighteenth century, blacks worshipped in the same churches as whites. But at the end of the eighteenth century, growing discrimination forced the establishment of separate black congregations. With the rise of separate churches many black community leaders and musicians emerged. Often the women made up the larger part of these congregations and choirs.

In the nineteenth century, during the transition from slavery to freedom, black Americans sought respect through intellectual pursuits. Music became important and young women, especially free middle and upperclass black women, learned to play the piano and sing, exhibiting the skills expected of their new social position.[41]

Just as white women musicians in Europe and the Americas began flourishing in the nineteenth century, so did black women musicians in the United States. These included singer Elizabeth Taylor Greenfield (1809-1876). Born of slave parents in Natchez, Mississippi, she received the name of her owner, Elizabeth Greenfield, a Quaker of Welsh descent who later freed her slaves and returned them to Liberia.[42] When Elizabeth refused to leave America, Mrs. Greenfield took her to Philadelphia where she studied music. She later performed in private recitals and parties. In 1851 she made her debut in a performance before the Buffalo Musical Association. It was this performance that established her reputation. During the years 1851-53 she gave concerts throughout the northern United States. The following year she toured England and sang at Buckingham Palace for Queen Victoria in a command performance. She received numerous press notices attesting to her remarkable talent and became known as "The Black Swan."

Marie Selika Williams took her operatic stage name, Madame Selika, from the opera *L'Africaine* by Meyerbeer. One of the most talented black concert artists of the late nineteenth century, she was one of the few black performers to have the opportunity for operatic training. After concertizing in the United States, Madame Selika toured Europe in the 1880s where she received excellent reviews in such newspapers as *Figaro* in Paris and the *Tagesblatt* in Berlin.[43] On her return to the United States, she eventually settled in New York as a vocal instructor at the Martin-Smith School of Music in Harlem.

The Hyers sisters of Sacramento, California also achieved singing fame. Their 1867 debut recital received much acclaim from the press. Their concert career included tours of the northern and western sections of the United States. In the 1870s they formed their own company and produced musical shows based on slavery themes.[44]

"Black Patti," Mrs. Sissieretta Jones (1868-1933), also ranked as one of the most famous opera singers of the late nineteenth century. She was born Matilda S. Joyner in Portsmouth, Virginia, and grew up in Providence, Rhode Island, where she studied at the Academy of Music in Providence. She later attended the New England Conservatory of Music in Boston.

Her concert career began at the Wallach Theater in Boston. She then toured South America and the West Indies. A performance at Madison Square Garden in New York led to a concert tour in cities throughout the United States. She performed at a White House reception given by President Benjamin Harrison in 1892. A successful year-long tour of Europe followed in which she became known as the "Black Patti," after the well-known Italian opera star Adelina Patti.

Upon her return she moved to New York and for the next nineteen years starred in the productions of an all-black company known as "Black Patti's Troubadours." The group appeared in many southern and western cities in the United States.[45]

In the twentieth century, black American women have begun synthesizing the music of their African heritage and European music.

Chapter Two

Florence Price
(1888-1953)

America's first black woman composer of international stature was born in Little Rock, Arkansas, only twenty three years after the Emancipation Proclamation had freed the slaves. Shortly after her birth in 1888, Florence Price's family moved to Chicago where her father, Dr. James Smith (the first black dentist to have an office on Main Street in Little Rock), became prominent with his own laboratory on the prestigious Loop.[1] He was a successful inventor and painter, winning cash prizes for his paintings and receiving royalties for his inventions. Her mother, Florence, was a talented soprano and concert pianist.[2]

Price's family nurtured her carefully as a child toward her ultimate role as a composer. By the early 1900s, she belonged to a select group of American symphonic composers and an even more distinctive circle of American composers who used the rhythms and melodies of the black American in their compositions. Price took her first piano lessons from her mother and showed promise as a performer. Later she also studied organ and violin. She attended elementary school in Chicago at Forrestville, but returned to Little Rock for high school.

In 1902, at age fourteen, Price graduated from high school and enrolled in the New England Conservatory of Music in Boston with a double major in piano and organ. She studied composition and counterpoint with Benjamin Cutter, George Chadwick from the New England School of Composers, and Frederick Converse (also a student of Chadwick). After discovering the world of music

31

composition, she was inspired to write her first string trio and symphony. She graduated with honors from the conservatory in 1907, receiving an artist diploma (for a five-year course), a teaching certificate, and a place of honor on the senior class program.[3]

Following her graduation, at age nineteen, she returned to Arkansas and began her career as a music educator at the Cotton Plant-Arkadelphia Academy in Cotton Plant, a school for blacks supported by a white northern church organization.[4] Here she met the white musician Neumon Leighton, a native of Cotton Plant. Interested in black musicians and composers, he had completed much research on their music and lectured frequently on the subject. Price met him at a lecture and, as their friendship grew, he began focusing his talks on her works. When she accompanied him to his lectures, he introduced her at the close of the sessions. Later, as voice instructor at a college in Memphis, Tennessee, (Southwestern at Memphis), he promoted her vocal works, especially the art songs, with student recitals.[5]

After one year, Price left the school at Cotton Plant. She taught briefly at Clark College in Atlanta, Georgia, and by 1912 had accepted a position in the music department of Shorter College in North Little Rock, Arkansas. In that same year she married Thomas J. Price, an attorney. They had a son, Tommy, and two daughters, Florence Louise and Edith. After Tommy died in childhood, she set Julia Johnson Davis's poem, To My Little Son, to music in his memory.

Price became a well-known music educator in Little Rock, and, in addition to teaching at Shorter College, she gave private violin, piano, and organ lessons. She found living in Arkansas unsettling, however. Several racial intimidations, characteristic of the South, involved her as a musician. In one such incident, she applied to the Arkansas Music Teachers Association; the association denied her membership because of her race.[6]

The Prices finally moved from Little Rock to Chicago in 1927, along with other prominent black families, after the lynching of a black man accused of assaulting a white woman; the man was hanged on a corner of the wealthy black neighborhood.[7] Price took advantage of the much wider opportunities for study in Chicago. She continued composing, performing, and teaching; she also studied composition with Carl Busch and Wesley LaViolette and orchestration with Arthur Olaf Andersen.[8] She attended the Chicago Musical College, Chicago Teachers College, Chicago University, Central Y.M.C.A. College, Lewis Institute, and the American Conservatory of Music where she studied with Leo Sowerby, a leading composer of organ music and anthems.[9] Price began publishing in 1928 with four pieces for piano, including a Mexican folk song.

In Chicago she also met and became a close friend of Estella C. Bonds, musician and mother of composer Margaret Bonds. "At one point," said Margaret Bonds later, "Miss Price was in such bad financial shape that my mother moved her into our house with her two children in order to relieve her mind of material considerations."[10] Estella Bonds was a generous woman with a wide circle of friends. Price became a part of her coterie of artists, musicians, and writers including Will Marion Cook, Abbie Mitchell, and Langston Hughes.

Margaret Bonds studied piano and composition with Price. Neumon Leighton later recalled: "Florence never tried to make Margaret copy her [Price's] style of composition. She heard and encouraged Margaret's concepts and style of composing."[11]

Price finally began achieving fame in the early 1930s when she won the Rodman Wanamaker Foundation Award for her *Symphony in e minor* and a piano sonata. The Foundation offered $1,000 in awards. Price received $500 for the symphony and $250 for the piano sonata. Her student, Bonds, won the other $250 for an art song. The *Symphony in e minor* had its world premiere on June 15, 1933, at the Chicago World's Fair. It was performed by the Chicago Symphony Orchestra conducted by Frederick Stock.[12] The program was broadcast; other performances followed. The Illinois Host House of the exposition presented Price in a program of her compositions. In the same year, she also performed her works for the International Council of Women. The Women's Symphony Orchestra of Chicago performed orchestral works by Price during the World's Fair and in 1934 Bonds appeared in their performance of Price's *Concerto in f minor* for piano and orchestra in a program devoted to women in music. Also in 1934, Price appeared as soloist in her own *Concerto in d minor* in the Chicago Musical College commencement program. This same work received another performance in Pittsburgh with Price as soloist.

In 1940 Eleanor Roosevelt attended a rehearsal of one of Price's symphonies. Impressed by the work, she cancelled her engagements in order to stay for the performance.[13] She later said:

> . . . They played two movements of a new symphony by Florence Price, one of the few women to write symphonic music . . . who has certainly made a contribution to our music. The orchestra rendered her symphony beautifully.[14]

On November 6, 1940, Price's *Symphony No. 3 in c minor* was premiered by the WPA Symphony Orchestra in Detroit, directed by Valter Poole. On the same program Price performed her *Concerto in One Movement*. She had one of her chamber works, a piano quintet, performed by faculty members of the Music School of the University of Illinois and the Forum String Quartet of Chicago.

Her reputation grew steadily. Sir John Barbirolli, British conductor and former director of the New York Philharmonic Symphony Orchestra, knew of her work and cabled her from England asking her to write a suite for strings based on black American spirituals. He presented the suite in Manchester, England.[15]

In addition to orchestral and chamber works, Price continued to write art songs, arrangements of spirituals, works for violin and organ, and piano etudes. She used the rhythms and melodies of the black idiom in such works as *Symphony in e minor*, *Concert Overture No. 1*, *Concert Overture No. 2*, *Three Little Negro Dances*, and *Negro Folksongs in Counterpoint* for string quartet. In *Symphony No. 3 in c minor*, she named the third movement "Juba" as a tribute to the African dances which inspired it.[16]

Price, probably through the influence of her teachers, Chadwick and Converse, preferred descriptive music. Her orchestral, chamber, and piano works were often programmatic. She based her art songs and choral works on descriptive poetry.

Although Price devoted most of her time to composing orchestral and chamber works, she found that publishers sought shorter pieces. (Unfortunately, most of the larger works remain in manuscript, today unavailable for performance. We do, however, have several of her published art songs, spiritual arrangements, and choral, piano, organ, and violin works.)

In her efforts to promote her music, Price gave manuscripts to such established and budding artists as Marian Anderson and Carol Brice. Marian Anderson included her *Songs to the Dark Virgin* on her second American concert tour. Three publishers—equally impressed by the work—asked to publish it.[17] Eugene Stinson, music critic of the *Chicago Daily News*, commented "*Songs to the Dark Virgin* was, as Miss Anderson (Marian) sang it, one of the greatest immediate successes ever won by an American song."[18]

G. Schirmer published the song in 1941. Price dedicated the work to her daughter, Florence L. Price. The text is by Langston Hughes, black American poet, author, and lyricist.

I   Songs to a Dark Virgin

Songs to a Dark Virgin is in a modified strophic form, with the same music for each stanza of the poem. Price begins each strophe or stanza with the same thematic material, but the second and third strophes vary in rhythmic and melodic treatment. The strophes are relatively short: the first has four lines; the second, five; and the third, four. In Price's setting the first strophe is six measures; the second, twelve measures; and the third, eleven measures.

The melodic treatment is simple and the harmony typical of the late nineteenth century. The overall design—A A' A''—creates enough contrast to provide variety without obscuring the original idea.

A one-measure introduction sets the general character of the accompaniment for the piece. Price uses a broken chord pattern in an ostinato-like (repetitive) pattern throughout. The term ostinato usually refers to a melodic idea or pattern that is constantly repeated. Here the term, ostinato-like pattern, is used to indicate the consistent and persistent repetitions found in the accompaniment pattern (Ex. 1).

These broken chords in sixteenth notes reflect the meaning of the sensuous words in the text. At the beginning of each strophe the

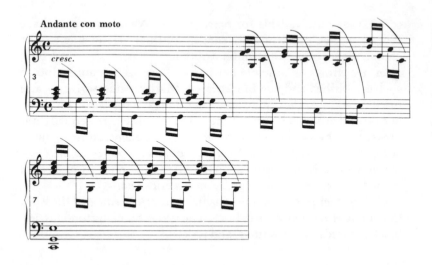

Ex. 1 *Songs to the Dark Virgin.* Meas. 3-4; 7, the broken chords and ostinato-like pattern of the accompaniment. Copyright 1941 G. Schirmer, Inc. Used by permission.

poet sees himself as (1) a jewel, (2) a garment, and (3) a flame. As the end of each strophe approaches, the poet's emotions overcome his descriptive powers and the voice reaches its highest, climactic point. As his excitement abates, the accompaniment slows down for emphasis and for a sense of resolution.

Word painting occurs in the vocal line in the second strophe for the words "might wrap about thy body" (Ex. 2). Later, in the same strophe, on the words "hold and hide thy body," the word "hold" appears as a sustained note over rich, startling harmonies. The harmonic progression here is not the chordal movement one would normally expect. However, this progression does reflect the text.

II   Other Art Songs

Price had other art songs published by such music companies as Gamble Hinged Music Company (*Moon Bridge*) in 1930 and Edward B. Marks Corporation (*Night* and *Out of the South Blew a*

Ex. 2 *Songs to the Dark Virgin.* Meas. 10-11, the folding line of the accompaniment depict the words "might wrap about thy body."

Wind) in 1946. In 1949, Handy Brothers Music Company published *An April Day.* She placed the text by Joseph F. Cotter in a simple musical setting. In a comfortably flowing style, she recalls a pleasant April day "when earth and sky and nature's world are clad in April's bliss." The form is strophic with a brief transition between the two strophes. This transitional section uses rapidly flowing broken chords, arpeggios, in the piano to paint the "balmy zephyrs" suggested in the text.

The phrases of the vocal line contain sustained tones at the beginning and end with evenly moving declamation within the phrases.

"On such a day as   this I think,"

This rhythmic movement depicts a comfortable balance of relaxation and activity.

The melodic range is just over an octave; at several points, the accompaniment doubles the vocal line with its rich chords. At the end of the first strophe, Price uses a series of chords made up of tones that are not related to the original key of the piece. This creates a chromatic progression leading to the transition. The accompaniment consists primarily of arpeggiated chords.

The dynamic shadings range from pianissimo to fortissimo. Each strophe begins somewhat loudly, builds to a forte in the first strophe, and reaches an exuberant fortissimo in the last strophe. In contrast, the transition, on the text about "balmy zephyrs," is piano to pianissimo.

The work ends with a descending arpeggio in double octaves for the piano against a sustained note in the voice.

III   Working in Black Idiom

Price frequently turned to the musical expressions of blacks for her compositions. She spoke the language of the black musical idiom with authority and blended it with the logic of traditional European music.

Price harmonized the melodies of raw folk material effectually and simply. Her vivid harmonic and rhythmic imagination, found in other works, served her well in arranging the folk song. Evidence of her talent appears in *Two Traditional Negro Spirituals* ("I am Bound for the Kingdom," and "I'm Workin' on my Buildin' ") published by Handy Brothers Music Company in 1949. Price dedicated these works to Marian Anderson who included them in her repertoire and recorded "I am Bound for the Kingdom" in her album *He's Got the Whole World in His Hands.*

Price wrote very simple chordal settings for both spirituals, allowing the melodies to dominate. The form of both songs is strophic with refrain (R). "I am Bound for the Kingdom" has only one verse (V) occurring between two refrains (R-V-R) while "I'm Workin' on my Buildin' " has two (R-V-R-V-R). In both songs each verse and each refrain is eight measures long.

Harmonically, both songs elaborate primarily upon one chord, the tonic, (built on the first note of a scale). There is a brief turn to the dominant (a chord built on the fifth note of a scale) which moves in the traditional way to the tonic to close each phrase, refrain, or verse. However, the verse of "I'm Workin' on my Buildin' " is richer harmonically because it has alternation between chords built on other scale tones and the tonic toward the end of the phrase.

"I am Bound for the Kingdom" is in G major and employs frequent chromatic colorations that are generally associated with the blues, such as the lowering of the third and seventh tones of a scale. Here, for example, Price uses three different forms of the seventh scale degree, F$^\sharp$. In measure 3 it appears as F$^\sharp$. In measures 4 and 5 she lowers it to F$^\natural$ and, finally, in measure 9 she assigns the singer a pitch between F and F$^\sharp$. In the first few measures of the verse, then, the voice uses both the raised and lowered seventh and an ambiguous seventh degree. (She omits the ambiguous seventh in the final cadence.)

Rhythmically, "I am Bound for the Kingdom" is direct and unsyncopated, except for the measure of $\frac{2}{4}$ inserted into the $\frac{4}{4}$ meter of the song just before the final "Glory in my soul" of the refrain. The change is small, but it adds emphasis to the concluding words.

The melody of "I'm Workin' on my Buildin' " is in F$^\sharp$ (natural) minor and is diatonic throughout the piece; it is based on the tones of the scale with no chromaticism. In the voice part, the seventh degree of the scale remains lowered until the final cadence where Price raised it to become a leading tone creating a more expected ending when it moves to the tonic.

The rhythm of this melody is syncopated. The motive associated with "I'm Workin' on my Buildin' " appears prominently in the refrain.

I'm a   workin' on my   buildin'

The verse uses a variety of syncopation at the beginning of each phrase as in "If I was a mourner."

If I was a   mourner

Price syncopates the first half of most of the measures of the song.

All of these devices and the use of the harmonies of the natural form of the minor scale give a folk style flavor to the composition.

My Soul's Been Anchored in de Lord is probably the best known of Florence Price's compositions. After Price had this spiritual for voice and piano published in 1937 by Gamble Hinged Music Company, she arranged it for voice and orchestra. Both arrangements appeared on recordings by several vocalists, including Marian Anderson and Leontyne Price.

Ex. 3 *My Soul's Been Anchored in de Lord.* Meas. 5-8; 17-20; 24-26, comparison of refrains and verse.

Fig. 1 Form of *My Soul's Been Anchored in de Lord.*

	FR	Verse 1 + BR	SR	Verse 2 + BR	SR	FR
No. of Meas.:	8	8	4½	8	4½	8

The most striking feature of this arrangement is the rhythmic setting. Price avoids duplicating the vocal line in the accompaniment. Syncopated rhythms contrast against even rhythms and the syncopation of both the melodic line and the accompaniment do not always coincide.

The piece is in strophic form with a verse and three different kinds of refrain: a full refrain (4 measures), a brief refrain (2 measures), and a shortened refrain (3 measures). The full refrain (FR) occurs at the beginning and end of the song. The brief refrain (BR) concludes each verse, and the shortened refrain (SR) follows the brief refrain as shown in Fig. 1. These verses and refrains are closely related melodically. The first half of each phrase is a variant of the other two, while the last half is a standardized cadential figure. The same melodic passage appears in the last half of each refrain. There are, however, no fewer than ten different harmonizations provided for the repetitious "My soul's been anchored in de Lord" phrase endings. Even the harmonic progressions that are similar (e.g., meas. 23 and 48) vary in spacing and voicing (Ex. 4).

IV   Choral Works

Price's interest in the musical portrayal of words through programmatic techniques also is evident in her choral works. Again, we see the influence of her teachers, Chadwick and Converse, and their nineteenth century European music tradition. (Programmatic effects were prevalent in the music of the Romantic and Post-Romantic eras.)

Price wrote and arranged choral works for the traditional mixed chorus as well as women's choruses. She usually selected her texts from descriptive poems, though at least one of her choral works is an arrangement of a spiritual.

Song for Snow, published by Carl Fischer, Inc., in 1937, is for mixed chorus with piano accompaniment. The lyrics by Elizabeth Coatsworth appeared originally in *The New Yorker Magazine* in 1934.

The poem divides into three sections. The first section (meas. 1–10) sets a winter scene of large expanses of snow: "The world is wider than in spring, the world is lighter than the air. . . ." The second section (meas. 11–28) introduces sleighs on the white roads and the sound of sleigh bells. The third section (meas. 30–40) begins with a nostalgic observation that the birds have migrated south and the leaves have fallen. This brief melancholy disappears with the realization that the mouths of the sleigh bells are singing trills like the birds and their leaf-like ears listen to the sound. Price sets the poem in ternary (A B A') form.

In the first section, the empty sound of open fifths in the accompaniment suggests the snow. Then we hear the principal motive, a light and airy theme outlining the G major tonic chord, in

Ex. 4 *My Soul's Been Anchored in de Lord.* Comparison of harmonizations of the final melodic cadence of refrain.

the soprano part (Ex. 5). The alto imitates it and the tenor slightly expands it. The tenors and basses give supportive chord tones. The static tonic harmony through most of this section contributes to the sense of tranquility created by a snowy landscape.

In the second section Price uses a conventional ostinato to imitiate the sound of trotting horses pulling the sleigh. Every two measures

The earth is ligh-ter than the sky,——— The world is wi-der than in spring,

Ex. 5 *Song for Snow.* Meas. 3-6, principal motive outlining the tonic chord.

she alternates melodic material between the soprano and tenor parts. The harmonic progression in this section becomes more adventuresome and the second half (meas. 18–28) ends with the ringing of the sleigh bells.

The beginning of the last section overlaps with the end of the second one for a smooth transition to the airy motive of the first section, but without the open fifths in the accompaniment. For the final cadence on the words "turn to the sound," she writes a very sonorous progression of low and mellow chords borrowed from the key of g minor. Although the composition is only two minutes long, it is able to depict the simple text.

Another of Price's choral works is *Moon Bridge* for three part women's chorus (SSA), originally published by Gamble Hinged Music Company in 1930 for solo voice and piano. The text is taken from a book of poems written by Mary Rolofson Gamble, mother of the owner of Gamble Music Company. Price arranged this work for women's chorus during the summer of 1950, and had it published by Remick Music Corporation.[19]

This nostalgic piece recalls childhood fantasies which see in the moon's rise from the silver bay a reflection on the water that makes a bridge between heaven and earth. On this bridge fairies come out to play and dance in jeweled robes. A miniature drama unfolds in the middle section where a mist appears to make the moon bridge disappear. All ends happily as the fairies glide away to their home in the rose tree's bowers and continue dancing.

Price's musical setting is quite direct with regular phrases of four measures in length and a simple A B A form. There is a short piano introduction, interlude, and a postlude.

The descriptive sections, such as the beginning, which tells how "the moon like a big round ball of flame rose out of the silver bay," are simple, triadic, and diatonic. But where the magical happenings occur, as in measures 17–18 where the poet "longed to stand on the magic bridge," the harmony becomes chromatic. For the most part the tonality is quite stable, the piece being principally in the key of F major. However, the middle section begins in the key of a minor.

V   Piano Etudes

Florence Price taught piano privately and, like the composers of earlier periods, she wrote and published numerous teaching pieces. She preferred the rhythms and melodies characteristic of the black idiom and used them in several of her piano etudes.

Three Little Negro Dances is a set of three short pieces for solo piano first published by Theodore Presser Company in 1933. Price also arranged the dances for two pianos. Later the publisher had them arranged for both standard and symphonic bands by Eric Leidzen. Major bands, notably the U. S. Marine Band, have played them.[20] The three titles in the set are "Hoe Cake," "Rabbit Foot" (both out-of-print), and "Ticklin' Toes." The tempi for all three pieces are fast with slightly different metronome markings in $\frac{4}{8}$ meter.

"Hoe Cake" is in three-part or ternary form (A B A') with an introduction. The syncopated melodic rhythm of the first section, , appears with a variation of articulation in the second

The melodic line has a rhythmic ostinato almost throughout the piece. In the A' section the melodic line moves to the left hand with a skeletal accompaniment in the right. The melody returns to the right hand in the second half of the section and another ostinato pattern enters the left hand accompaniment. The melodic material in section B has the same general rhythmic and motivic character as in the A sections but with changes in pitches and octave placement to provide contrast.

"Rabbit Foot" is the slowest and least syncopated of the three pieces. This is also the shortest of the three, with only 48 measures.

Fig. 2 Form of "Rabbit Foot" from *Three Little Negro Dances.*

Section	A	B	A	A'	Codetta
No. of measures	8 + 8	4 + 4	8	8	8
Key	F	g minor	F	F	F

Ex. 6 "Rabbit Foot" from *Three Little Negro Dances.* Meas. 1-2; 17-18, contrast of tonality with similar motivic figures. Copyright 1933 Theodore Presser Company. Used by permission.

Written in the key of F, this piece is in ternary form with a codetta (Fig. 2).

It has much melodic repetition, as do all of the pieces in the set. The B section motivic material is basically the same as that of the A section, with a sudden change to chords from the key of g minor. Even though the melodic motive of A is visually obvious, the change of harmony hides it aurally (Ex. 6).

Price changes the close harmony of the A section to open harmony in the A' section. That is, the spacing of the chord tones is wider and more sparse. At the codetta, chromaticism enters the harmony.

"Ticklin' Toes" is a lively and rhythmically syncopated piece in the key of C. The prominent rhythm,

varies only slightly. The form is ternary with a codetta (Fig. 3).

The A sections are the most strongly unified rhythmically and harmonically. In the B section, each of the eight-measure phrases presents a new idea. The effect is tuneful and rhythmic. In order not

Fig. 3 Form of "Ticklin' Toes" from *Three Little Negro Dances.*

Section	A	B	A	Codetta
No. of measures	8 + 8	8 + 8 + 8	8 + 8	8

Fig. 4 Outline of *Three Little Negro Dances*

Title	Key	Form	Tempo	Features	No of meas.
"Hoe Cake"	C	Ternary with introduction	Allegro M. M. =120	prominent syncopated rhythms. ostinato throughout.	68
"Rabbit Foot"	F (g minor) F	Ternary with codetta.	Allegretto M. M. =120	hidden motivic treatment.	48
"Ticklin' Toes"	C	Ternary with codetta	Allegro M. M. =138	prominent syncopation. 3 different ideas in B section.	64

to detract from these elements, the harmony is mostly tonic and dominant with little chromaticism.

Fig. 4 compares the key, form, tempo, features, and number of measures for the three dances.

Price continued her composition and concert careers in Chicago until her death there in 1953 following a lengthy illness. She left behind a music that, as we have seen, blends elements of the black idiom with European music. She established an international reputation as a composer that places her with her black male contemporaries William Dawson and William Grant Still. Her vision of black and European music inspired many black women composers, mostly notably Margaret Bonds.

Chapter Three

Margaret Bonds

(1913–1972)

Margaret Bonds's musical genius seemed destined for success from her birth in 1913 in Chicago. She came from a prominent, creative family that drew major artists of the time into their home. Her mother, Estella C. Bonds, was an accomplished musician in Chicago with a coterie of friends that included artists and humanitarians of all races and religious backgrounds. Bonds met all the living composers of African descent and in her childhood and youth she became close friends with sculptor Richmond Barthe, poets Countee Cullen and Langston Hughes, soprano-actress Abbie Mitchell, and composers Will Marion Cook and Florence Price.[1]

Bonds had read most of the work of Hughes before they first met. Both black artists found they had much in common and became close lifelong friends. Through Hughes and others like him she immersed herself in black literature and dedicated herself completely to the "black experience."[2] For some of her inspiration, she turned to such works of Langston Hughes as *The Dream Keeper* and "The Negro Speaks of Rivers." At her request, he wrote the libretto for her cantata *The Ballad of the Brown King*.

Abbie Mitchell introduced her to some of the world's vocal literature. The daughter of a black mother and Jewish father, Mitchell was a renowned performer of lieder and French art songs as well as the music of composers of African descent. She taught

Bonds "the importance of the marriage between words and music which is demanded if one is to have a song of any consequence."[3]

Will Marion Cook led her toward a more popular type of composition. Bonds wrote later:

> ... and when composers like Will Marion Cook had an opportunity to present a Negro choir on NBC, I was sent to extract all of his choral parts, which, incidentally, he changed daily. Even now, when I write something for choir and it's jazzy and bluesy and spiritual and Tchaikowsky all rolled up into one, I laugh to myself, "That is Will Marion Cook."[4]

Cook advised her: ". . . get right into the heart of Negro inspiration . . . Go where the Negro creates."[5] Bonds followed his words and from serious black poetry, European art songs, and Afro-American popular music, fused a personal style.

Bonds studied piano with her mother when barely out of infancy. After she revealed innate musical talents, her mother envisioned a career as a concert pianist for her. Her compositional gifts, however, were apparent early and eventually took preeminence. She composed her first song at age five. During a visit to a family friend, she announced that she had composed a song called "The Marquette Road Blues."[6] "Of course," recalled the friend Ruby Clark later, "the piece was not written down but she played it proudly for us."[7]

Bonds began her serious musical apprenticeship in high school. While attending Parker High School in Chicago, she began to study composition and piano with Florence B. Price and composition with William Dawson. Bonds often helped Price copy parts for composition contest deadlines. She worked closely with various singers, such as Etta Moten and family friend Abbie Mitchell, and played for the rehearsals and dance routines of Muriel Abbott, a well-known dancer, in the Empire Room of the Palmer House in Chicago. When black composers, such as Noble Sissle, Dawson, and Cook had works performed in Chicago, she often copied parts. The inspiration and knowledge gained through these experiences greatly influenced her work with the black idiom.

In high school she also joined the National Association of Negro Musicians (NANM), an organization that promotes the cause of black music and musicians. She became a charter member of the Junior Music Association organized in the mid-1920s.[8] Bonds worked so effectively for the organization that musician and former president Theodore Charles Stone praised her, saying that she "represented all that is stated in the purpose of the NANM."[9]

After high school, she entered Northwestern University in Evanston, Illinois, to continue her musicial studies. She became more and more interested in the creative process. Musical ideas seemed to flow with such urgency that she recorded them immediately. She composed continuously. She even wrote while riding the train to and from school each day, at times jotting down ideas on the edges of magazine pages.[10] At the age of twenty-one, she completed both the bachelor of music and master of music degrees at Northwestern.

In the early 1930s, Bonds opened a school in Chicago for ballet, art, and music called the Allied Arts Academy. Because of the Depression the school did not succeed.[11] In 1939, she moved to New York for further study and to pursue a career as composer-pianist. Bonds had confidence in her musical talents and did not hesitate in her commitment to black music.

She worked for a short time as an editor for a music company where her duties also included composing for people who could not write their own music. Harry Revel, a well-known Hollywood writer, was among the musicians whose work she edited. She was successful, beginning in 1939, in publishing many of her popular songs, including "Peach Tree Street" (for the movie *Gone With The Wind*), "Georgia," and "Spring Will be so Sad." On the first two she collaborated with Andy Razaff and Joe Davis and on the last, with H. Dickinson. "Peach Tree Street" and "Spring Will be so Sad" appeared on recordings by such artists as Glenn Miller, Charley Spivak, Woody Hermann, and The Three Suns.[12]

In 1940, Margaret married Lawrence Richardson, a probation officer with the Supreme Court in New York, and had a daughter, Djane, named after Djane Herz, her piano teacher at Juilliard School of Music.

At Juilliard, she also studied piano with Henry Levine and composition privately with Roy Harris, Robert Starer, and Emerson Harper, whose wife Toy encouraged her dedication to the "black experience."

When Bonds showed her work to the world-renowned composition teacher, Nadia Boulanger, she found that Boulanger liked *The Negro Speaks of Rivers*, a setting of the Langston Hughes poem, and many of her other compositions. Boulanger acknowledged that Margaret Bonds "had something," but she refused to take her as a student because she did not understand how to develop Bonds's talent. She told Bonds that she should continue composing as before and advised her not to study with anyone or to study fugue."[13] Bonds later felt that Boulanger's genius as a teacher was quite evident in her refusal to accept her as a student because in her style, a combination of European techniques and black improvisation so strongly prevailed that further study of European traditions might have stifled her.

Bonds found great joy in composing and nothing disturbed her while she wrote. She often worked late into the night and at odd moments. For example, when she took her daughter to dancing class she would work on a score while the other mothers exchanged gossip.[14]

She was interested primarily in developing the black idiom into larger musical forms so she incorporated either spiritual melodies or original melodies in spiritual style into her works. Her compositions are often very pianistic and, in many instances, are difficult to perform. When reproached about their complexity, she refused to alter the music, saying it would compromise her principles as a composer.[15] Many of the accompaniments in her spiritual arrangements reveal these intricacies. The melodic lines are simple but the accompaniments complement, not duplicate, with a counterflow of ideas against the melodic line. However, even with the complicated rhythmic and syncopated accompaniments, simplicity dominates.

Bonds's compositions included art songs, choral works, orchestral works, piano pieces, and popular songs. Many are in the repertoires of several leading artists such as Betty Allen, Carol Brice, Eugene Brice, McHenry Boatwright, Adele Addison, Todd Duncan, Hortense Love, Charlotte Hollman, Theodore Charles Stone, William Warfield, Martina Arroyo, and Leontyne Price, who often commissioned Bonds to write special spiritual arrangements for her. Bonds's lifelong friend, Hortense Love, commissioned her to arrange five spirituals collected from the music of the Creek-Freedmen. The Creek-Freedmen are a mixture of Creek Indian and Negro.[16] Love performed these five spirituals at her Town Hall debut in New York

Bonds obtained wide theater experience in New York and formed the Margaret Bonds Chamber Society which presented concerts featuring black musicians and the works of black composers. In addition to composing, she pursued simultaneous careers as concert pianist, private piano teacher, and church musician. She worked tirelessly toward each musical goal.

As a concert pianist she performed in Canada and the United States with appearances as guest soloist with the Chicago Symphony Orchestra, Chicago Women's Symphony Orchestra, the Scranton Philharmonic Orchestra, and the New York City Symphony Orchestra. On a program given by the Chicago Women's Symphony devoted to women in music, she performed Price's *Concerto in f minor*. She also appeared on radio programs in New York, and on Mary Astor's Showcase, CBS radio, in Hollywood. Bonds gave concerts in Orchestra Hall in Chicago and Town Hall in New York City. As a member of duo-piano teams she toured with her piano students Gerald Cook and Calvin Jackson as well as Frances Kraft Reckling. They appeared both in concerts and in such nightclubs as New York's Cafe Society, Spivy's Roof, Cerutti's, and the Ritz Tower, and at the Jai-Lai in Columbus, Ohio.

Margaret Bonds had begun a private teaching career in Chicago, and continued to teach piano in New York because she felt teaching was an important part of her career. She taught at the American Theatre Wing and served on the staff of Stage for Youth in New York. Later, she taught both piano and music theory at the Los Angeles Inner City Institute. She also devoted her time to lecturing about her music, black music, and black musicians. She believed strongly that black children should understand their heritage . . . and develop an appreciation for music.[17]

When Dr. Monroe A. Wall, pastor of the Mt. Calvary Baptist Church in Harlem, asked her to improve the music of his church, she readily agreed because of her religious and musical convictions. She designed a program to teach the reading of music and sight-singing because she felt that this was especially important for young blacks. She thought they should learn music systematically.

Bonds was one of the few women to find wide acclaim in her own lifetime. She received numerous scholarships, fellowships, and awards, including the National Association of Negro Musicians Scholarship, Rodman Wanamaker Award in Composition, Julius Rosenwald Fellowship, Roy Harris Fellowship, Honor Roll of Most Distinguished Negro Women of the Century (Illinois Centennial Authority), and ASCAP Awards, 1964–66. In 1967 she received the alumni medal from Northwestern University.[18] Other Northwestern alumni honored at the same honors convocation were former U.S. ambassador to the United Nations, Arthur Goldberg; Sen. George S. McGovern; and actress Patricia Neal.[19] She felt that this recognition was especially important because it represented progress toward her lifelong goals: the establishment of the black idiom in the arts and the unbiased acceptance of the black artist. She could recall vividly that when she had attended Northwestern University during the Depression years, she had been one of a few black students. At that time, the university had denied them free access to several facilities because of their race.

In 1967 she moved to California to work in films and other musical projects. She became associated with the Inner City Cultural Center and served as teacher and musical director until her sudden death on April 26, 1972.[20]

I   The Negro Speaks of Rivers

When singer-actress Abbie Mitchell introduced Bonds to works by black composers, "Ethiopia Saluting Colors" by Harry T. Burleigh impressed her. She later wrote about the experience:

> In my teens and highly impressionable I began unconsciously to copy Harry T. Burleigh. In a basement of the Evanston Public Library I found works of a poet named Langston Hughes. I was intrigued by his first published poem "The Negro Speaks of Rivers." I myself had never suffered any feelings of inferiority because I am a Negro and I had always felt a strong identification with Africa, but now here was a poem which said so many different things I had known and was not able to verbally express. Burleigh's "Ethiopia Saluting

Colors" became Margaret Bonds's "The Negro Speaks of Rivers."[21]

After Bonds set the Hughes poem and played it for him, she showed her composition to one of her teachers who thought it too extreme and told her to remove the "jazzy augmented chords." She refused the advice, believing God had guided her, an early reflection of her deep theological convictions.[22]

Bonds gave the song to Marian Anderson, and, though Anderson was very polite, Bonds felt that the "jazzy augmented chords" frightened her.[23] Anderson never sang this setting; later, she performed a more somber setting by Bonds's contemporary, Howard Swanson. In 1942, Handy Brothers Music Company published the piece. It was originally written for solo voice and piano but later Bonds arranged it for mixed voices and piano.

The poem is freely written in a mixed prose and poetic style, describing the vast areas of the world inhabited by black men, as identified by their historical rivers—the Euphrates in Asia Minor, the Congo in Africa, the Nile in Egypt, and the Mississippi in North America. The music is through-composed (without repetition), changing with the historical and geographical references. A river motive is the major unifying musical element. At the beginning, the piano gives the motive in a bare form (Ex. 7).

Later, full harmony and exotic arpeggiated chords transform the motive to depict the Euphrates (Ex. 8).

The empty harmonies of parallel octaves and fifths represent the Nile. Bonds consciously planned the left-hand chords in measures 39–48 to represent pictorially the pyramids mentioned in the text[24] (Ex. 9).

The composition closes with the same river motive in a low, rather muddy register (Ex. 10).

Ex. 7 *The Negro Speaks of Rivers.* Meas. 1-2, river motive.

Ex. 8 *The Negro Speaks of Rivers.* Meas. 23-24, transformation of river motive to depict the Euphrates.

Ex. 9 *The Negro Speaks of Rivers.* Meas. 41-42, the pictorial representation of the pyramids in the left-hand chords.

Ex. 10 *The Negro Speaks of Rivers.* Meas. 74-77, final statement of river motive.

II   Three Dream Portraits

Margaret Bonds selected three poems by Langston Hughes for her *Three Dream Portraits*, a set of three songs for voice and piano published by G. Ricordi in 1959. She wrote one of the songs, "Dream Variation," for Adele Addison and the other two, "Minstrel Man" and "I, Too," for Lawrence Winters, singers associated with the New York City Opera Company.

The three poems depict related segments of the American black experience. The first, "Minstrel Man," is the grimmest as it contrasts the minstrel man's gay facade with his inner feelings. The second and third, however, are full of hope, exploring feelings of being black and expressing irrepressible good humor in adversity. "Dream Variation " is expansive; the imagery is first energetic: "fling," "whirl," and "dance," and then calm: "rest," and "night coming tenderly, black like me." "I, Too" is confident, proud, and patriotic without chauvinism. The three poems show a progression from despair and resignation to hope—a mirror of the reality of black life in America from the early 1900s until the late 1950s. Langston Hughes originally published the poems in 1932 in a collection called *The Dream Keeper;* Bonds chose these three and placed them in a way that would reflect changing attitudes.

The settings do not relate musically. We might try to relate them by their forms, which are all essentially strophic, but she has given us three different interpretations of strophic form. In "Dream Variation" the vocal parts of both strophes are quite similar, but in "I, Too," we have a freely improvised restatement of the first strophe.

"Minstrel Man" is between these two structurally. The first half of each strophe is nearly identical in both melody and accompaniment, but the second half of each vary considerably. Only the prominent use of long, sustained tones on words like "pain," "long," "known," and "die," show the relationship of the two parts. The work is a series of mood paintings with many characteristics of the jazz style.

The first song, "Minstrel Man," begins in c minor with a syncopated ostinato that sounds like weary ragtime. Just before the voice enters, however, the mode changes to C major as the minstrel man puts on the wide grin he habitually uses to greet the audience. In spiritual-like style, each short phrase of the text ends with a long tone sustained for at least a measure until the next phrase begins. At the end of the strophe the sustained tones lengthen to twice their former value.

Tonally the entire composition is in c minor; harmonically it is rich and complex. Bonds uses many altered chords—secondary dominants and Phrygian relationships. Sevenths, ninths, and elevenths, appear as do thirteenth chords which suggest polyharmonies, one chord in the right hand and another in the left. Progressions are often unusual as in measures 12–13 where a dominant seventh has a deceptive resolution to a D♭ major harmony built on the lowered second degree of the C scale. This alteration suggests a sudden shift to the Phrygian mode, which has a half step between the first two tones instead of the whole step found in major and minor scales (Ex. 11). The progression is further complicated by the F♭ major appoggiatura (ornamental) chord spelled E(F♭) A♭ C♭ in the right hand in measures 13–14 that resolves to D flat major. The progression of roots by thirds, such as this between F♭ and D♭, is a favorite of Bonds. It is a common root relationship in both spirituals and late nineteenth century European music.

Another interesting progression occurs at the end of the first strophe (Ex. 12). Here Bonds writes a minor dominant (a chord with

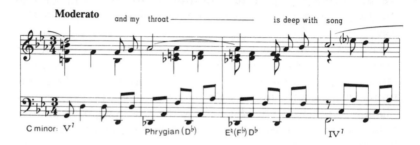

Ex. 11 "Minstrel Man." Meas. 12-15, unusual progressions and Phrygian relationships.

suf – fer ——————— af–ter I have held my pain —————— so long

V⁷
(minor dominant)
VI
(A♭major chord)
V¹³/V
V
I
(tonic)

Ex. 12 "Minstrel Man." Meas. 19-23, ornament to emphasize the word "suffer"; overlapping and altered harmonies.

a lowered seventh scale degree), a typical feature of black music from spirituals to New Orleans jazz. The voice gives emphasis to the B♭ and the word "suffer" with an ornament. In the next measure the left hand of the accompaniment changes to an A♭ major chord (VI in c minor), while the right hand continues the fifth (D–G) of the preceding chord. Thus, instead of progressing conventionally in blocks, the harmonies overlap. In measure 21, the chord is basically a dominant thirteenth of the dominant. This chord (a V¹³ in the key of G) ordinarily would be spelled D F♯ A C E G B, probably omitting several of the tones, such as the fifth, ninth, and eleventh. Bonds, however, uses them all either in a harmonic or melodic capacity, some with alteration. A becomes A♭ (in the voice), E become E♭, and B becomes B♭. The major third, F♯, is colored by the addition of F♮ in the right hand of the piano. In the next measure, still accompanying the word "pain," Bonds again gives both the major (B♮) and the minor (b♭) third of the chord. Finally, we reach the tonic in measure 23 at the end of the first strophe. Within the strophes she avoided the tonic. Thus, Bonds enriched the simple melody with harmonic imagination.

The song "Dream Variations" reflects the simplicity of the poem. The second stanza is a close variant of the first expressing the same thoughts and feelings but with changes of detail. For example, "white day" becomes "quick day," and the neutral thought "to dance" becomes imperative—"Dance!" Bonds responds to this poem with strophic form for the vocal part. Not bound by a text, the piano accompaniment to the second strophe differs markedly from the first in melody, harmony, rhythm, and texture. Here, then, we have the unusual example of a vocal part in strophic form with a through-composed accompaniment.

"Dream Variation" (27 measures) is less active rhythmically than the other two songs. The slower tempo and the rocking movement of the accompaniment set a tranquil mood for the dreaming suggested by the text.

Probably in allusion to dreaming, the tonality of this composition is more ambiguous than that of "Minstrel Man." The key signature of four sharps implies E major or c# minor. The voice, however, begins in G major as shown in Ex. 13. The first two measures of the melody are pentatonic (a scale using only five tones). Here Bonds uses only the tones G A C D E, leaving the sustained tones on "sun" (F#) and "dance" (B) in measures six and seven, fresh and dramatic as they fill in the gaps of the G scale. In the beginning measures of the accompaniment, parallel quartal chords (chords built in fourths) embellish a conventional V^9 harmony followed by two measures of tertian harmony (triadic—chords built in thirds). Throughout the song Bonds mixes quartal with tertian harmony to support the dream theme of the text.

The first strophe ends in E major. The chord progression of the strophe does not follow the traditional pattern of root relationships by ascending fourths and descending fifths. Instead, often the root relationships are by step, third, and tritone (an augmented fourth).

Bonds shows her preference for the third related progression near the end of the second strophe. The progression reflects a relaxed mood by drifting from c# minor to A major and back, then changing suddenly to C# major and continuing on through A and F major as illustrated in Ex. 14. This passage, simulating the feelings expressed in the text, lacks the tension of other passages in Bond's songs.

Finally, another interesting harmonic subtlety concerns the use

Ex. 13 "Dream Variation." Meas. 4-7, the ambiguity of key and pentatonic beginning of the melody.

of parallel sevenths in the first part of the piece for harmonic coloring. The progression is related not to any particular part of the text, but rather to the progression of parallel quartal chords that the composer uses periodically throughout the song. Near the end of the song, the parallel sevenths change to octaves, giving a sense of resolution.

"I, Too" (41 measures) is the most aggressive, dynamically and rhythmically, of the three songs. There is a variety of rhythmic

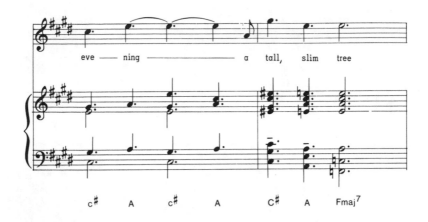

Ex. 14 "Dream Variation." Meas. 22-23, use of third relationship related progression for a relaxed mood and drifting effect.

patterns in this very syncopated piece, including triplets in both quarter note and eighth note patterns.

In this song Bonds concerns herself with the intricacies of melodic variation, for the melody of the second strophe is a very free, quasi-improvisatory variant of the first (Ex. 15). The two parts begin alike and meet occasionally on single notes, but in between these occurrences, the second part differs widely from the first. Ex. 15 shows the two strophes.

Bonds apparently kept certain notes of the first strophe in mind as meeting points and improvised on them in the second half, keeping their relative position in the strophe the same. In principle, this is the same procedure used by jazz musicians like Louis Armstrong or Duke Ellington to improvise on a well-known tune like *When the Saints Go Marching In* or *Mood Indigo*. Here, however, this is Bond's original tune.

Simpler harmonically than *Minstrel Man* and *Dream Variation*, the song has more triads and open chords. The second strophe is dominated by a harmonic-rhythmic ostinato that repeats for ten measures (Ex. 16).

Ex. 15 "I, Too." Comparison of the two strophes.

Bonds deliberately adapted an unchanging ostinato as the accompaniment. This allows all of the performer's and listener's attention to focus on the unfolding vocal improvisation. In addition, the harmonic background includes chords suggestive of blues harmonizations.

This piece is one of the clearest examples of her employment of improvisational compositional techniques, one of the unique characteristics of black composers. Traces and suggestions of it appear in her other music as well.

The setting of the text "But I laugh" reveals another interesting

Ex. 16 "I, Too." Meas. 19-20; 25-26, ostinato of final strophe.

Ex. 17 "I, Too." Meas. 15, the musical representation of the words "But I laugh."

facet of Bond's compositional technique—word painting. The accompaniment literally laughs in staccato and syncopated eighth notes as shown in Ex. 17. Bonds avoids a rather obvious and unconvincing reference here by working the laughter motive briefly in the end of the introduction and then again in the concluding section. In the body of the song, the motive appears in a four measure development as a concluding section for the first strophe. Instead of being a passing and whimsical exercise in literal word painting, the motive is an essential part of the song.

Omitting the final line of the poem in her musical settting, Bonds leaves the basic purpose of the poem unexpressed. Instead, the same material of the introduction returns to end the song.

III   I Got a Home In That Rock

Bonds held deep religious beliefs and dedication to the black experience. She arranged spirituals both for solo voice and for choir. At least one of the spirituals she arranged contained a text that represented her basic theology—*I Got a Home in that Rock.*

She arranged this spiritual for voice and piano and for voice and orchestra, dedicated it to the vocalist Betty Allen and had it published by Mercury Music Corporation in 1968.

She gave the traditional spiritual a dramatic setting, raising it from comparatively simple beginnings to the realm of art music. Whether or not the piece loses some of its spontaneity depends upon the performer. Bonds takes the four-verse text and builds the energy of each verse to the climactic last strophe which promises the destruction of evil by "fire next time".

The melody is quite simple and repetitive. Each phrase is four measures in length as represented below.

a		a'		b		a
4	+	4	+	4	+	4

The beauty of the melody lies in its simplicity and its unceasing fervor as the pitch rises in each of the first three successive phrases from the comparatively calm and low statement that "I got a home in-a that Rock," to the cry on a high F, "Between the earth and sky—Know I heard my Saviour cry," then back to the low calm original statement "You got a home in-a that Rock, don't you see." Bonds writes an accompaniment that complements rather than distracts from the slow syncopation of the principal melody. Harmonically, the accompaniment consists of widely spaced chords featuring tenths in the left hand and a free-voiced texture in the right hand. In some measures the chords are thick—from six to eight notes each. In others they form simple four-part harmony. The texture of the accompaniment reflects the intensity found in the text. Therefore, the most complex, emphatic statement appears in the last strophe: thick chromatic chords back up "God gave Noah the rainbow sign, can't you see, no more water but fire next time, Better get a home in that Rock, can't you see." In very effective word painting, slowly ascending chords in the right hand accompany the words "God gave Noah the rainbow sign."

For the piece, Bonds uses polychords, quartal harmony, and both major and minor forms of chords, a characteristic suggestive of jazz-blues styles. The work ends dramatically with a penultimate $D^\flat$ major chord and a descending scale leading to a final F major chord.

IV   Black Idiom in Larger Form

Bonds commissioned Hughes, her close friend, to write on the subject of Jesus Christ's birth and the fact that one of the three wise men, Balthazar, was dark-skinned. He responded with *The Ballad of the Brown King*, a plain, direct, and eloquent libretto.

The original composition, shorter than the final published version, was premiered on December 12, 1954, in New York City. After that performance, Bonds shelved the manuscript and forgot about it until the civil rights movement and Dr. Martin Luther King, Jr.'s work brought it to her attention. She deeply admired King's successful direction of the Montgomery, Alabama, passive resistance movement and his non-violent philosophy. Her earlier interest in the heroism of Martin Luther, champion of religious freedom for the Germans, strengthened her respect.[25]

Certain interesting associations exist between Balthazar and King. Balthazar was a dark-skinned wise man who was a king; Martin Luther King was a dark-skinned wise man named King, who led blacks in America. Moreover, both King and Balthazar took part in the birth of a new socio–religious movement.

The Westminster Choir of the Church of the Master performed the completed work in New York City and CBS televised it on "Christmas U.S.A.," December 11, 1960.[26]

Bonds originally scored *The Ballad of the Brown King* for chorus, soloists, and orchestra. Sam Fox Publishing Co. published it in 1961, with the orchestral part reduced to piano score. The work consists of nine movements. The text presents the traditional Christmas story but focuses on Balthazar, the brown wise man. Mixed chorus is the predominant ensemble, forming the basis of seven of the nine movements, used either by itself (movements 2, 3, 8) or with soprano, alto, tenor, or baritone soloists (movements 1, 4, 6, 9). Movement 5 is for men's chorus and Movement 7 is for women's chorus.

For this cyclic work, Bonds drew from the spiritual, jazz and calypso rhythms, blues, and folk styles. She also used techniques from the European musical tradition, especially those found in opera, i.e., the quasi-recitative material and the imitative passages.

The first movement, *Of the Three Wise Men*, for tenor solo and chorus begins with a piano introduction which sets the mood of the work. The melodic line is based on the pure form of the f minor scale, suggesting an exotic Eastern atmosphere. The minor mode changes to the major mode during the first six measures (f minor to the relative A♭ major). This alternation between F and A♭ occurs throughout this movement. The relationship of keys used is close: f minor—A♭ major—F major.

The tenor solo announces the subject of the cantata in the style of a minister reading a sermon text. The solo is very brief, only four measures long, both in the beginning and near the end of the movement.

The chorus follows the soloist, singing a slow moving legato pattern in the upper three voices (SAT). This material is in a choral or chorale style—an example of the European influence. The basses sing a contrasting eight-note staccato pattern dividing the second and fourth beats of each measure. The choral section echoes and expands upon the melodic and textual material of the opening tenor solo. The movement ends with a return of the introduction as a postlude for the piano.

We can see the jazz influence in the second movement, *They Brought Fine Gifts*, with her use of widely spaced seventh chords, parallel tenths, quartal harmony, syncopated rhythm, and suggestions of syncopation. The seventh chords, used in succession, appear primarily in the vocal parts with countermelodic material in the piano accompaniment. This slow movement is for mixed chorus and is more somber than the first. It ends with descending ninth chords moving in half steps and a final quartal chord. The chorus sustains this chord over a piano accompaniment based on the introduction of the movement.

The third movement, *Sing Alleluia,* for a cappella mixed chorus is in a spiritual style. The predominant characteristics are simple four-part harmony with traditional progressions, repetitive patterns, and a limited melodic range. The form of the movement is strophic. This is the shortest movement with only eight measures, which are repeated once.

The fourth movement about the birth of Jesus, *Mary Had a Little Baby,* is in a ternary form with the following scheme:

Fig. 5 Form for *Mary Had a Little Baby*

Introduction	A Soprano Solo	B Chorus	A Chorus & Sop. Solo	Postlude

Bonds combines contrasting rhythms reminiscent of calypso song styles. For example, the basic accompaniment rhythm appears against the soprano solo rhythm

In the final A section, sopranos and altos add an even rhythm as an obbligato accompaniment. The movement ends with the voices in four-part harmony and a brief piano postlude based on the solo.

The fifth movement, *Now When Jesus Was Born,* is for men's chorus and has an introduction based on the introduction of the first movement. Here, however, the rhythm varies, with slower note values.

The form of this movement is binary with an asymmetrical structure. In the first section, the tenors and basses sing four lines of the text in a straight-forward narrative in octaves. The second section consists of the last line of text sung in harmony in response to the first section. A modest, but effective key scheme reflects the text. The movement begins in c natural minor for a subdued and lightly oriental sound to underscore the text's announcement of Jesus' birth. Bonds uses the new key of F major for the arrival of the wise men from the East. Finally, for the last section in which the wise men announce they have seen the star, she returns to the key of C but in a major rather than a minor mode.

The first section is mildly dissonant with the voices singing a relatively simple legato melodic line in unison against a repetitive pattern in the accompaniment. The dissonance results partly through the suggestion of ninth and eleventh chords.

In the second section the mood changes. The voices enter with a lyrical legato idea in triadic harmony with new accompaniment. The vocal lines in this section move in a step-wise fashion in contrast to the more disjunct quality of the first section. The accompaniment pattern is repetitive with only slight variations.

The sixth movement, *Could He Have Been an Ethiope?*, scored for baritone solo, tenor solo, soprano and tenor duet and mixed chorus, again draws upon the first movement material for the introduction.

The baritone solo uses exactly the same pitches found in the opening melodic idea from the first movement introduction. Phrases generally end with upward inflections to indicate the questions presented in the text in a quasi-recitative style related to opera. The recitative is used when dialogue of some length needs to be presented in a manner similar to speaking. Later, a brief section in dialogue style does occur.

Bonds uses an imitative passage in the choral material to reemphasize the speculation of the solo text. The altos present a one measure motive imitated in the next measure by the sopranos, followed by the basses presenting the same bewildering statement in the following measure.

The seventh movement, *Oh Sing of a King Who Was Tall and Brown*, for women's chorus, resounds with rhythm and energy, clearly the most dynamic section in the work. The form is strophic with an introduction and piano interlude as presented in the figure below.

The piano introduction begins in a very jazz-like style. The vocal

Fig. 6 Form of *Oh Sing of a King Who Was Tall and Brown.*

Section	Introduction	Strophe 1	Interlude	Strophe 2
Medium	Piano	Voices and Piano	Piano	Voices and Piano
No. of Meas.	16	22	8	35

parts, in contrast, are more subdued rhythmically and are in three-part harmony. The use of triplets and downward two-note slurs are indicative of blues and jazz.

A piano interlude, based on material found in the first and sixth movements, precedes the second strophe. The movement ends with a slightly varied and shortened restatement of the material of the first strophe.

The eighth movement, *That Was a Christmas Long Ago*, is short, only 17 measures long, and is for mixed chorus. The text is a recapitulation. This movement draws its musical ideas from the first and second movements. The introduction is an exact repetition of the introduction of the second movement and the vocal material is similar to that of the first movement. Although it is not so marked, this movement is actually a transition to the final movement.

The last movement, *Alleluia!*, is for soprano and alto duet and mixed chorus. The text praises Christ as the King.

The movement begins softly with a repeated $A^\flat$ in the basses and piano for two measures. To this, the tenors and altos add alternating f minor and $B^\flat$ major triads. The basses drop the $A^\flat$ in measure 3 but it is continued as a pedal (the same note repeated or held regardless of the movement above it) in the accompaniment to measure 20.

The alternating chords and the $A^\flat$ pedal serve as an accompaniment to both the syncopated alto solo and the duet, a repetition of the alto solo in two-part harmony.

The next section is rhythmically intricate. The tenors sing a legato "Alleluia" in half notes while the basses sing a staccato "Alleluia" in an eighth note pattern on the second and fourth beats, ideas taken from the first movement. The women's voices have a contrasting syncopated rhythm in three parts against the material of the male voices.

A lengthy piano interlude based on this complex material leads to a new section, again derived from the first movement. The cantata closes with the chorus singing in unison the legato "Alleluia" previously sung by the tenor voices while the accompaniment continues the material of the interlude. The final measure is a full chorus (four-part) statement of "Christ the King" syncopation immediately following a dramatic measure of rest.

Fig. 7 shows the medium, form, and keys of each movement of *The Ballad of the Brown King.*

Shortly before her sudden death in 1972, Bonds reached another high point in her relentless drive to synthesize black music and European music. The Los Angeles Symphony Orchestra, conducted by Zubin Mehta, premiered her *Credo* for chorus and orchestra.[27] She had never doubted herself as a composer because her family and leading black artists of the early twentieth century recognized and encouraged her musical genius from childhood. Yet, this premiere assured her that one of her deepest desires, the acceptance of the black musician, was perhaps possible.

Fig. 7 Outline of *The Ballad of the Brown King.*

Movement Tempo No. of meas.	Medium	Form and/or Character	Keys Used (in order)
1. *Of the Three Wise Men* = 108 67 meas.	Tenor Solo with Mixed Chorus	Strophic	f A♭ F A♭ F
2. *They Brought Fine Gifts* = 84 40 meas.	Mixed Chorus	Through-Composed	A♭
3. *Sing Alleluia* = 80 8 meas. (repeated)	Mixed Chorus (a capella)	Choral interjection	E♭
4. *Mary Had A Little Baby* = 100 52 meas.	Soprano Solo and Mixed Chorus	Strophic 1st strophe— solo (interlude chorus) 2nd Strophe— solo and chorus	E♭

Continued on next page

Fig. 7 Outline of *The Ballad of the Brown King.*
(Continued)

Movement Tempo No. of meas.	Medium	Form and/or Character	Keys Used (in order)
5. *Now When Jesus Was Born* = 69 83 meas.	Men's Chorus	Binary (verse — refrain)	c F C
6. *Could He Have Been an Ethiope* = 69 109 meas.	Baritone Solo; Soprano and Tenor Duet and Mixed Chorus	Through-Composed	f (F) f (g) d D
7. *Oh, Sing Of A King Who Was Tall and Brown* = 104 81 meas.	Women's Chorus	Strophic form, with a piano interlude between strophes	C
8. *That Was A Christmas Long Ago* = 80 17 meas.	Mixed Chorus	Transitional	A♭
9. *Alleluia!* = 80 85 meas.	Soprano and Alto Duet and Mixed Chorus	Binary (verse — refrain)	A♭

Chapter Four

Julia Perry
(1924-1979)

Julia Perry's major contribution to American music is her eclectic musical language. She drew upon the heritage of black music but she also assimilated the dissonant and unconventional harmonies of the twentieth century from such teachers as Nadia Boulanger and Luigi Dallapiccola.

When Perry was born in 1924, black musicians had established themselves. William Grant Still and Harry T. Burleigh were composing classical music, and W. C. Handy, and Eubie Blake were writing popular music.

During her childhood, the family moved from Lexington, Kentucky, to Akron, Ohio. She studied violin with the intention of becoming a violinist but later she became interested in piano and voice. Mable Todd, her voice teacher in Akron, strongly influenced her sensitive musical personality.[1]

After graduating from high school in Akron, Perry attended Westminster Choir College in Princeton, New Jersey, where she received a bachelor's degree at age 23 and master's degree at 24. She studied piano, violin, voice, conducting, and composition. Although she showed the greatest talent in composition, she found conducting to be her most rewarding medium of performance. In addition to the satisfaction of the performance itself, she used the voices and instruments to experiment and to study the musical effects of her own compositions. Her experience training and conducting a young choir in Birmingham, Alabama, during the summer before her senior year was very rewarding: at the end of the summer, the choir included one of her works on a program. She continued to pursue choral music and wrote a secular cantata, *Chicago*, for her master's thesis. It was based on poems by Carl Sandburg and scored for baritone, narrator, mixed chorus and orchestra.[2]

In 1948 Perry moved to New York City and studied composition at the Juilliard School of Music, while continuing to compose. In 1950 Perry served as assistant coach and participant in the Columbia Opera Workshop. In the same year her sacred cantata *Ruth*, for mixed voices and organ, had a performance at the Riverside Church in New York on April 16. (Later, in 1954, the McMillan Theatre at Columbia University produced her one-act opera, *The Cask of Amontillado*.) By this time, she had two published works: *Carillon Heigh-Ho* in 1947 and *Lord, What Shall I Do* in 1949.

In the summer of 1951 she studied at the Berkshire Music Center at Tanglewood with Luigi Dallapiccola. In 1952 she received a Guggenheim Fellowship and studied composition with Dallapiccola in Florence, and with Nadia Boulanger in Paris. She also received the Boulanger Grand Prix at Fountainbleau for a viola sonata.[3] In 1955 she won another Guggenheim and made her second trip to Europe to study with Dallapiccola. She also studied conducting during the summers of 1956, 1957, and 1958 with Adone Zecchi and Alceo Galliera at the Accademia Chigiana in Siena, Italy.[4]

In 1957 Perry conducted a concert tour sponsored by the United States Information Agency in several European cities. These concerts received much acclaim from European critics, especially in Siena, Rome, and Genoa.

Back in the United States, Perry continued to compose and teach until illness forced her into early retirement. She taught at Florida A & M University in Tallahassee in 1967, and in 1969 she served as a visiting music consultant at the Atlanta Colleges Center.[5] In 1964 she won the American Academy and National Institute of Arts and Letters Award, and in 1969 she received Honorable Mention in the ASCAP Awards to women composers for symphonic and concert music.

We know little about Perry's last years. She lived in Akron, Ohio, in seclusion and died there on April 29, 1979.

Perry's music is eclectic. She uses twentieth century compositional techniques which range from the mildly dissonant but traditional harmonies of her early works to the more dissonant and unconventional harmonic structures of the later ones. Her works, which include arrangements of spirituals, symphonies, chamber music, choral anthems, operas, and art songs indicate her remarkable organizational ability as a composer. Even with the apparent unorthodox character of some of her music, such as *Homunculus C. F.*, a chamber work for percussion, harp, and piano, she adapts a logical structure to frame the unconventional.

She composed *Homunculus C. F.* during the summer of 1960. It was written in her apartment, located on the top floor of her father's medical office building in Akron, Ohio, which "was equipped with all of the necessary facilities except a piano." These clinical surroundings evoked memories of the medieval laboratory where Wagner, youthful apprentice to Faust, made a successful alchemy experiment, fashioning and bringing to life a creature he called *homunculus*,[6] a Latin word for "little man"—a test tube man. Perry selected percussion instruments for her simulation of a test tube creation; then, maneuvering and distilling them by means of the Chord of the Fifteenth (C. F.), brought this musical test tube baby to life.[7] Although it is pure speculation, C. F. may also stand for *Cantus Firmus*, a fixed or given melody used as the basis for a work. This is a term that Perry certainly understood, and that accurately describes the role of her "Chord of the Fifteenth."

She builds the chord on an E root. Ex. 18 gives the intervallic structure.

Perry establishes the chord with a D$^\sharp$ although a D$^\natural$ occurs frequently in one section of the work. The chord, built from a succession of superimposed thirds, is actually the simultaneous combination of two major-major seventh chords (the root, third,

Ex. 18 Intervallic construction of the Chord of the Fifteenth (C. F.).

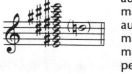

augmented	15th
major	13th
augmented	11th
major	9th
major	7th (minor 7th)
perfect	5th
major	3rd

and fifth comprise a major triad and the seventh is a major interval) as shown in Ex. 19. In describing the work, which does not belong to any conventional major or minor key, Perry calls it a "pan-tonal" composition. The work is scored for standard percussion instruments: 4 timpani, large and small suspended cymbals, 2 medium cymbals, snare drums, bass drum, large and small woodblocks, xylophone, vibraphone, celesta, and piano and harp.

The composition consists of four sections. The first section is entirely rhythmic, using only the non-pitched percussion instruments. The second section is principally melodic; the third principally harmonic; the fourth a combination of the melodic, rhythmic and harmonic elements (see Fig. 8).

Section I begins with a rhythmic canon between the snare drum and the large woodblock. In the rhythmic canon, the second 4 measures are the retrograde of the first 4 measures (Ex. 20). The imitation continues to measures 15–16 where both instruments stop playing. The first twenty measures of the canon actually serve as an introductory passage. A little more than halfway through this section the bass drum enters with an ostinato-like counterrhythm. At the end of the rhythmic canon the bass drum varies its rhythm slightly as the two cymbals enter to close the introduction. In the second half of section I the rhythms are nearly identical with those in the first half. Here she changed the notation of the snare drum rhythm from a single dotted quarter note to a thirty-second note followed by a doubly dotted eighth note for greater emphasis (Ex. 21). A transitional passage begins at measure 41 with melodic material presented by the timpani. The melodic pattern makes use of the 3rd, 7th and 9th of the C. F., and is presented monophonically. The snare drum and woodblock interrupt the pattern twice. This transition features an overlapping of the rhythmic and melodic material and leads to the second section.

Ex. 19 Two major-minor seventh chords, combined in the Chord of the Fifteenth.

Fig. 8 Outline of *Homunculus C.F.*

Section	Meas.	Presentation of C.F. Tones	Features
I Rhythmic	1-40	none	entirely rhythmic
transition	41-60	D# G# F#	introduces melodic elements. alternates with rhythmic.
II Melodic	61-80	E F# G# D#	duet between timp. and harp.
Melodic	81-94	B E G# F#	new motive presented and developed heterophonically.
III Harmonic	95-105	E F# B G# D#	based on E7 or E9 chord throughout section
IV Combined	106-180	E G# B D# F# A# C# E# (D)	D (not in C.F.) alternates with D# entire C.F. presented (M.177)

Ex. 20 *Homunculus* C. F. Meas. 1-8, snare drum part, the second four measures are a retrograde of the first four measures.

Ex. 21 *Homunculus C. F.* Meas. 1-2; 21-22, snare drum part, the the change of dotted rhythms between the two halves of section I.

Section II, the melodic section, begins with a duet between the timpani and harp introducing the fundamental tone of the C. F. (E) and its enharmonic equivalent (F$^\flat$). The pattern used in this duet also includes the 3rd (G$^\sharp$), 7th (D$^\sharp$), and 9th (F$^\sharp$) of the C. F. Although this is a primarily melodic section, the harmonic element is anticipated with the introduction of a chord by the harp. Then the celesta, vibraphone, and harp present a new motive based on the root (E), 3rd (G$^\sharp$), 5th (B), and 9th (F$^\sharp$) of the C. F. and develop it heterophonically. Large and small woodblocks punctuate the melodic material with a slightly syncopated pattern.

Section III, the harmonic section, begins with sustained tones in the celesta and vibraphone. The motive of the melodic section becomes absorbed and obscured as it combines with chords presented between the various parts. Three measures after section III begins, the harp enters and there is rapid movement in the other instruments. Perry based this entire section on E^7 or E^9 chords which further supports the basis of the composition—the C. F. built on E.

Section IV, the final section, gradually combines the rhythmic, melodic, and harmonic ideas. The section opens with melodic-rhythmic motives similar to those found in sections I and II. Though the harmonic element is present in the harp, it does not become prominent until later in the section. There are fast-moving rhythmic motives in the pitched percussion instruments in a quasi-ostinato fashion. Each instrument plays certain notes of the C. F.—xylophone: E, B, D; vibraphone: B, F$^\sharp$, D; celesta: G$^\sharp$, A$^\sharp$. It is interesting to note the use of a D in the xylophone and vibraphone instead of the D$^\sharp$ of the C. F. More tones of the C. F. are added (C$^\sharp$—harp and vibraphone; E$^\sharp$—xylophone). At this point the chord tones gradually build up in arpeggiated fashion until the C. F.

emerges finally in its entirety at measure 177. The intensity increases through rise in pitch, textural changes, faster tempo, repetitive rhythmic and chord patterns, along with an increased dynamic level, to a climactic and abrupt ending.

This work, based on tones of the Chord of the Fifteenth, has one exception in the D♮ found in the last section. The timpani establish E as the fundamental tone of the chordal structure in the duet with the harp in section II. Perry reinforces this in the third section which is based solely on E⁷ or E⁹ chords. The tones of the C. F. appear for the first time in the composition in the following order:

7th	3rd	9th	root	5th	11th	13th	15th
D♯	G♯	F♯	E	B	A♯	C♯	E♯

"The Homunculus," in Goethe's *Faust*, "a spirit or an idea or an archetype seeking realization, is searching for a way to break from his test-tube phase and to come into being."[8] Faust learns that "one must approach the ideal by degrees, repeating nature's own process."[9] The logic of the formal structure of this work and the gradual construction of the Chord of the Fifteenth suggest an attempt to represent the idea of growth indicated in Perry's statement concerning the metamorphosis of her "musical test tube baby"—*Homunculus*.[10]

Perry wrote both text and music for *Song of Our Saviour* published by Galaxy Music Corporation in 1953. Written for the Hampton Institute Choir, Hampton, Virginia, it is for unaccompanied mixed chorus.

Tonally, the anthem is in the Dorian mode, a scale represented by the white keys on the piano from D—D. The word mode refers to scales prevalent during the Middle Ages. In this work Perry has transposed the Dorian mode to A.

The anthem is a miniature variation form as shown in the figure below. Each variation is increasingly more intricate rhythmically.

Perry based most of the anthem on an ostinato that is an expanding intervallic succession in two parts of one measure duration. Hummed by altos and tenors, it remains in the background as the sopranos enter with the principal melody (Ex. 22). This soprano melody, incidentally, reveals many of the characteristics of a spiritual. It is repetitive; in the four measure tune, the first three measures

Fig. 9 Variation Form of *Song of Our Saviour.*

Section:	Introduction	A	A'	A"	B	Interlude (intro.)	A	A'
No. of Measures:	2	9	7	8	10	2	9	7

Ex. 22 *Song of Our Saviour.* Meas. 1–3, the primary ostinato of the work.

repeat the same motive over and over, until a new cadential passage appears at the end of the fourth measure. This repetition, in addition to the repetition of the ostinato, creates an almost hypnotic effect until the ostinato is augmented (note values increased) so that its length is two measures instead of one in section A'. It still accompanies the same melody which has no rhythmic change. In addition, a new ostinato appears in the bass, also wordless (Ex. 23).

The text of the first section depicts the scene of Jesus' grave as Joseph offers flowers and Mary says a prayer. In the A section the solo melody presents the text. The entire A' section is wordless until the final phrase "and breathed a prayer" sung by the solo voice. All the way to this last part the harmony is conventional and static,

Ex. 23 *Song of Our Saviour.* Meas. 12-13, augmented ostinato in altos and tenors with new ostinato in basses.

following the orderly progression of the ostinato. But, the end of this section suddenly shifts to an F♯ minor chord on the final word of the solo text, "prayer," with prominent cross relations between F and F♯ and a simultaneous clash of C and C♯. It is a confused progression, bringing to an end a well-controlled section.

In the next section, A″, the tempo increases (poco piu mosso), and the tenors sing a quick, new motive of one measure duration to the text "Jesus was born in a manger lowly" answered by a slower-moving, calm reply by the basses—"child of Bethlehem." The sopranos sing the same material with an answer by the altos. Here Perry incorporates the typical call-response principle of the spiritual into a composed anthem. The new call-response ostinato continues while the original ostinato disappears; this change of ostinato allows the original ostinato to sound fresh upon its reappearance.

The alternation of the ostinato between the male and female voices continues into the next section, B, with one exception. The sopranos sing new material, an interjection resembling the shout style used in spirituals. The interjection "Glory Hallelujah" occurs every two measures until, in the last phrase, all voices sing it. The end of the section overlaps with the return of the introduction, now an interlude, and section A. The work ends with a repeat of the A' section and the contorted progression discussed.

I Spirituals

Julia Perry's works include arrangements of several spirituals. Among them are *Free At Last* and *I'm a Poor Li'l Orphan in this Worl'*. In the May, 1951, issue of *Musical America* a reviewer said of her *Free At Last* that Perry "set the melody with taste and appropriate simplicity."[11] This can be said of most of her spirituals. She focuses conscious attention on the melodic line and avoids bulky or opaque accompaniments.

Free At Last, a freely arranged spiritual published by Galaxy Music Corporation in 1951, is for solo voice and piano.

The piece is in strophic form with a Verse-Refrain structure as shown in Fig. 10.

The spiritual is in F major and begins with a brief melodic introduction for the piano. It anticipates the vocal line with a prominent syncopated rhythm, associated with the text "Free at last."

The vocal line of the refrain is simple, syncopated, and somewhat repetitive. The melody outlines a tonic triad like a trumpet-call signalling freedom. Perry pairs this with a slowly moving accompaniment in conjunct parallel sixth chords in the right hand and a tonic-dominant pedal in the left hand, creating a contrast with the syncopated, disjunct melody (Ex. 24). The first verse is in d minor and the "Free at Last" syncopated rhythm appears in almost every measure. The parallel movement of the accompaniment resembles that of the first refrain but changes from chords to a two-voiced pattern moving against a D pedal.

The accompaniment of the second verse continues the ostinato-

Fig. 10 Verse-Refrain Structure of *Free At Last.*

Section	Intro-duction	Refrain	Verse 1	Refrain	Verse 2	Inter lude	Modi-fied Verse	Refrain
No. of Meas.	2	10	10	10	10	2	8	21

Ex. 24 *Free At Last.* Meas. 23-24, contrast between the syncopated, disjunct melodic line and the conjunct chords of the accompaniment.

like parallel pattern in the left hand, and Perry varies this pattern to create a countermelody in the right hand (Ex. 25). The counter-melody occurs with the first and third phrases of the verse while the second and fourth phrases, "I thank God I'm free at last" (taken from the refrain), has the same parallel chordal accompaniment used in the refrain. A two-measure interlude leads to the modified verse. In this interlude the introduction pattern of parallel chords in the right hand become tenths in the left hand.

The first four measures of the modified verse present an interesting combination of the melody and parallel chordal accompaniment of the refrain against new vocal material that is similar to the vocal lines of verses one and two. The new material begins to dominate for the last four measures. The accompaniment abandons the refrain material and becomes supportive again. These eight measures are majestic; a ritardando prepares for the final refrain.

The last refrain varies at the beginning with an octave displacement of the first note of the vocal line, and the accompaniment has large chords on the first and last beats for two measures. The singer repeats the last phrase to end the refrain and the spiritual. Here, in *Free at Last*, Perry has taken a simple repetitive tune and created a short dramatic setting.

Ex. 25 *Free At Last.* Meas. 33-34, the ostinato-like parallel pattern of the left hand against a countermelody in the right hand and vocal melody.

She had *I'm a Poor Li'l Orphan in this Worl'*, arranged for solo voice and piano, published by Galaxy Music Corporation in 1952. The melody is slow and plaintive. Simplicity dominates and Perry chose a very uncomplicated, bare accompaniment. The form is strophic, and each verse consists of three repeated lines and a refrain (a–a–a–R).[12]

Written in e minor, the accompaniment elaborates upon one chord, the tonic, in the first and third verses. At the end of the third line of each of these verses, the music turns briefly to the dominant and then back to the tonic for the refrain line. The first and third verses have basically the same accompaniment pattern, a widely spaced, sustained, broken-chord for one measure followed by simple two-note chords in the right hand (Ex. 26). The second verse accompaniment is a single line counter-melody creating a polyphonic texture in contrast to the homophonic texture of the first and third verses. An E major (picardy third) chord ends the piece.

The setting is entirely diatonic with a modal character, a treatment that underscores the simplicity of the folk song style.

Ex. 26 *I'm a Poor Li'l Orphan in this Worl'*. Meas. 1-3, one chord accompaniment pattern using a widely spaced, sustained broken-chord and simple two-note chords.

II   A Larger Work in the Contemporary Idiom

Julia Perry composed *Stabat Mater* in 1951 and dedicated it to her mother. This work, which launched her career, has received numerous performances in both Europe and the United States.

The *Stabat Mater*, a sequence of the Roman Catholic liturgy which did not survive the Council of Trent, was restored to the liturgy in 1727. It became a sequence for use in the office of the Seven Sorrows of the Blessed Virgin Mary (September 15). The Church also uses it for two other liturgical occasions: the Friday before Second Passion (Palm Sunday) and as the "Hymn of the Compassion of the Blessed Virgin Mary" during Lent.[13] Among the many composers who have set this famous text to music are Josquin, Palestrina, Pergolesi, Haydn, Rossini, and Dvorak.

Stabat mater dolorosa, a Latin poem attributed to the thirteenth century Franciscan Jacopone da Todi, is set in ten double versicles or couplets. Because of the double versicles, many settings have involved antiphonal writings or double choruses. Palestrina used two choruses and combined several couplets which suggest larger musical units. Composers of the seventeenth and eighteenth centuries produced large works for chorus and orchestra, in which the text often consisted of many autonomous and characteristically differentiated movements.[14] The settings of the nineteenth century composers leaned toward more elaborate works with characteristics of operatic style. They divided the poem variously into sections either by individual or double versicles. Josquin and Palestrina separated their works into two main sections; Pergolesi used twelve sections (the last section ends with an "Amen" chorus—*Presto assai*). Haydn's setting is in thirteen sections. Rossini and Dvorak set theirs in ten sections. The works are for five voices (Josquin), double chorus (Palestrina), two solo voices (Pergolesi), or mixed chorus and soli (Haydn, Rossini, and Dvorak).

Perry's text does not agree, in several instances, with the current text in the *Liber usualis*.[15] In many cases her text corresponds more closely to those used by Rossini and Pergolesi. Other changes reflect the personal preferences of Perry.

For instance, she changes both words and letters, primarily vowels. Versicle 8 of the original Latin poem begins *Vidit suum dulcem natum* which Perry changes to *Vidit Jesum dolcem natum*. Other changes include *moriendo desolatum* to *morientem desolatum* in versicle 8; *cordi meo valide* to *corde meo valide* in versicle 11; and, in versicle 19, *Morte Christi* to *Morte Christe* (see text on pages 87-89). Perry apparently considered euphony and repetition of vowel sounds and consonants more desirable than linguistic accuracy.

The text, with translation by Perry, provides a musically dramatic setting, filled with emotion. In her vocal conception of this work, she reaches for pathos. At times, the work borders on the operatic.

A number of musical similarities exist between Perry's work and the settings of Pergolesi and Rossini. Her setting is particularly close to Rossini's in the use of word painting and orchestral devices. We will discuss the specific similarities later.

The scoring of Julia Perry's *Stabat Mater*, for contralto and string orchestra or string quartet, is similar to Pergolesi's setting for solo voices (soprano and alto) and string orchestra. Perry divided the setting into ten sections with two versicles to each section, but this differs from both Pergolesi and Rossini who grouped the versicles in a less regular pattern (see Fig. 11). Even with the ten sections indicated in the score, the work divides, aurally, into two large sections (Part I—versicles 1-8; Part II—versicles 9-20, similar to the arrangement found in Josquin's setting). In Part I the poet describes the scene and circumstances of the Mother Mary weeping at the foot of the cross on Calvary. The poet, in very poignant language, depicts the sorrow of Mary and the suffering of Jesus. In Part II the language becomes more personal as the poet asks the Mother Mary to allow him to share in her sorrow.

Perry's work is cyclic in that the opening motive (introduction) recurs at various points throughout the composition. The work is generally dissonant and tonal.

Fig. 11 Comparison of Versicle Grouping in the *Stabat Maters* of Pergolesi, Rossini, and Perry.

Versicle	Pergolesi	Rossini	Perry
1	I Duet	I Chorus and Quartet	I All movements for alto solo and orchestra
2	II Soprano aria	II Tenor aria	
3	III		II
4	IV Alto aria		
5	V	III	III
6	Duet	Soprano duet	
7		IV	IV
8	VI Soprano aria	Bass aria	
9	VII Alto aria	V Bass	V
10	VIII Duet	recitative & chorus	
11	IX	VI	VI
12	Duet	Quartet	
13			VII
14			
15			VIII
16	X	VII	
17	Alto aria	2nd Soprano	IX
18	XI	VIII	
19	Duet	1st Soprano and chorus	X
20	XII Duet	IX Quartet	
	Presto Assai "Amen"	X Chorus Finale	

Text of Stabat Mater
with translation by Julia Perry

Part I

Stabat Mater dolorosa	Stood the Mother sadly weeping
Juxta crucem lacrimosa,	1 Near the cross her presence keeping
Dum pendebat Filius.	Whereon hung the Only Son;
Cujus animam gementem,	Through whose spirit sympathizing,
Contristatam et dolentem,	2 Him she saw in sorrow and compassion
Per transivit gladius.	Through whom passed the cruel sword.
O quam tristis et afflicta	O how mournful and afflicted
Fuit illa benedicta	3 Was this favoured and most blessed
Mater Unigeniti.	Mother
	Of the Only Son;
Quae *morebat* et dolebat,	Through His dying, suff'ring, grieving
*Et tremebat** cum videbat	4 As she trembled scarce perceiving
Nati poenas inclyti.	Pains of the Illustrious One.
Quis est homo qui non fleret	Who the man who could not weep
Christi Matrem si videret	5 Saw he there the Mother of Christ
In tanto supplicio?	In great supplication?
Quis non posset contristari,	Who could not give consolation
Piam* Matrem contemplari,	6 To the Mother contemplating,
Dolentem cum Filio?	Mournful with her child?
Pro peccatis suae gentis	For the sinning of His people,
Vidit Jesum in tormentis,	7 Saw her Jesus in great torment
Et flagellis subditum.	Beaten with scourger's rod;
Vidit *Jesum dolcem natum*	Saw her Sweet One dying
*Morientem** desolatum,	8 Yes, forsaken, crying
Dum emisit spiritum.	Yield His spirit up to God.

Part II

Eia Mater, fons amoris,	Tender Mother, fount of love,
Me sentire vim doloris	9 Let me feel thy sadness,
Fac, ut tecum *luguem.*	That with thee my tears shall flow;

Fac ut ardeat cor meum	Make my heart so steadfast for Him, O
In amando Christum Deum,	10 Mother
Ut sibi complaceam.	Make it burn with love for thy Son,
	That I may be pleasing unto Him.

Sancta Mater, istud agas,	Holy Mother, this be granted:
Crucifixi fige plagas	11 Let His wounds be firmly planted
*Corde** meo valide.	In my heart forevermore,

Tui nati vulnerati,	See the Saviour wounded,
Tam dignati pro me pati,	12 Depths unbounded for me suffered;
Peonas *meam* divide.	Pangs of grief me divide.

Fac me *verum* tecum flere,	Make me weak with thee in union
Crucifius condolore,	13 At the crucifix, there condoling;
Donec ego vixero.	I shall help to bear the blame:

Juxta crucem tecum stare,	Near the cross with you standing,
Te libenter* sociare	14 Sharing freely agony with Him
In planctu desidero.	Forever, forever: this I desire.

Virgo virginum praeclara,	Virgin, of all virgins dearest,
Mihi jam non sis amara:	15 Be not bitter when thou hearest
Fac me tecum plangere.	Make me with thee to weep.

Fac ut portem *Christi* mortem	Make me bear the death of Christ
Passionis *ejus sortem,**	16 His passion sharing shamefully
Et plagas recolere.	While renewing pains in me.

Fac me *plagas* vulnerari,	Wound for wound be there created
Cruce *hac** inebriari,	17 By the cross intoxicated,
Ob *amorem** filii.	For love of thy Only Son.

*Inflammatus et accensus,**	Here inflam'd I stand in the fire of love.
Per te Virgo, sim defensus	18 Through thee, virgin protect me
In die judicii.	On the judgement day.

Fac me cruce custodiri,	Of Thy cross, Lord, make me keeper
Morte Christe praemuniri,	19 Of Thy cross, Lord, defender
Confoveri gratia.*	With a grateful heart to Thee
Quando corpus morietur,	When the body death has riven,
Fac ut animae donetur	20 Grant that to the soul be given
Paradisi gloria. Amen.	Glories bright of Paradise.

Punctuation follows the *Liber Usualis*, pp. 1634–37. The words underlined differ from those in the *Liber Usualis* either in spelling or in the word itself. Underlined words followed by an asterisk (*) follow Rossini's text.

A slow, solemn introduction begins the work. The cellos and basses announce the subject, followed by freely imitative entrances of the viola and violin II. This theme resembles in contour the theme used in the Pergolesi and Rossini settings. The similarity is in the use of the descending appoggiaturas (a musical ornament with an auxiliary note dropping to an adjacent note) found in each of the melodies. The general direction and shape have resemblances as well. Each of these lines begins with an ascending movement turning to a descending movement. Each motive appears first in a low voice and then freely imitated in a higher voice. The distance and interval of imitation vary. In Pergolesi's setting the distance is two beats (one half measure) at the interval of a second; in Rossini's the distance is twelve beats (two measures) at the interval of an octave; in Perry's the distance is six and one half beats (one and one half measures) at the interval of a third (Ex. 27).

Violin I provides a brief pizzicato accompaniment figure and then a short cadenza-like solo, with an improvisatory character, based on the introductory motive. Open fifths on G and D anticipate the opening interval of the vocal line. This introductory section suggests the tonality of D. The voice enters with a relatively stepwise, almost mournful, melody to present the first versicle. The melody includes suggestions of improvisation which support the weeping portrayed in the text. The melody is dissonant against the sustained two-note accompaniment. The return of the opening motive is imitative and serves as a transition to the second versicle. An e

Ex. 27 *Stabat Mater.* Comparison of first movement motives.

minor ostinato (violas and violin II) with the major third (G#) in the cellos and basses and a change in meter signal a new vocal line and the beginning of versicle 2. The rhythm is more animated in this versicle. The accompaniment continues the e minor ostinato. The versicle ends, "through whom passed the cruel sword," and Perry sets the text with a disjunct vocal line in the style of a dry recitative to end the section.

No real break occurs between the first and second sections. A solo violin presents the thematic material for the second section (versicles 3 and 4) with a diminished fifth in the violas. The theme of the violin solo, with its ascending movement and dotted rhythm, is similar in general contour to the opening theme used by Rossini for the tenor aria in the second section of his setting (Ex. 28). The vocal line is very lyrical and somber and reverses the two halves of the melodic idea presented by the violin. An E pedal continues through the setting for versicle 3.

The accompaniment changes to a pizzicato ostinato for solo cellos in versicle 4. The E pedal returns and an e minor tonality appears and continues until the end of the section.

Section three (versicles 5 and 6) is mournful and mysterious. It has a faster tempo (allegro) and more rhythmic activity than the previous sections. The section begins with a rhythmic variation of the main motive from section one. After the orchestra develops this

Ex. 28 *Stabat Mater.* Similarities of general contour and rhythm of second section.

motive a repeated descending appoggiatura anticipates the vocal entrance.

The contour and intervals of the vocal line are strikingly similar to the vocal line in Rossini's duet as shown in Ex. 29. Resemblances also exist among the vocal line in versicle 6 in all three versions (Ex. 30). The contour of each line is similar and on the whole, the most prominent intervals are the second and third. The violas play a doleful countermelody against the vocal line in measures 90–96, which is supportive of the commiseration expressed in the text. The dissonance between the voice and accompaniment is more pronounced in this section. The faster tempo and the agitated treatment of material, both vocal and instrumental, contribute to the intense dissonance.

In section four (versicles 7 and 8) the high level of dissonance continues. The general mood is one of agitation representing the drama inherent in the text. Throughout the section an arpeggiated ostinato based primarily on descending and ascending fourths gives a quartal harmonic effect. The accompaniment figure resembles the accompaniment of versicle 7 in Pergolesi's work as shown in Ex. 31. At measures 111–112, versicle 8, a dotted rhythm appears in an otherwise smooth vocal line. It is interesting to note that Rossini also used a dotted rhythm for the vocal line of the same versicle (Ex. 32).

A whole-tone scale (a scale consisting of whole steps only) at

Ex. 29 *Stabat Mater.* Comparison of third movement vocal lines.

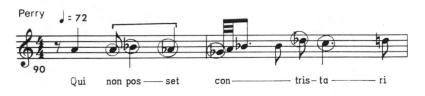

Ex. 30 *Stabat Mater.* Comparison of vocal line for versicle 6.

Ex. 31 *Stabat Mater.* Comparison of accompaniment
figures in versicle 7.

Ex. 32 *Stabat Mater.* Comparison of dotted rhythms used for versicle 8.

measures 117–118 (violins) adds further to the vagueness of tonality already created with the quartal harmony. An increase in the agitated rhythmic activity—rising lines, trills, and tremolos—create the climactic feeling that concludes Part I of the work.

Section five is quieter and more tonally stable than the previous sections. Perry yields to the demand of the text, which also changes in mood and character at versicle 9.

A simple, unaccompanied vocal line, with a modal quality, opens the section. The voice presents a Dorian melody on A. Perry treats the voice and instruments antiphonally to reinforce the pleading nature of the poet's requests. This close imitation between the vocal line and the accompaniment ends at measure 141 where the instruments provide a contrasting answer signalling the entrance of versicle 10. The answer gradually overlaps with the vocal line.

Section six (versicles 11 and 12) begins with imitative entrances of the instruments. The ascending motive becomes an ostinato accompaniment heard throughout the section either in imitation or in one of the instruments alone. The intervals of the vocal line resemble the intervallic structure used by Rossini in his setting for the same versicle as shown in Ex. 33.

Another intervallic similarity exists between Perry's vocal line at measures 168–169 (versicle 12) and Rossini's setting as shown in Ex. 34.

Ex. 33 *Stabat Mater*. Comparison of intervallic structure used for versicle 11.

Ex. 34 *Stabat Mater*. Comparison of intervallic structure used for versicle 12.

The opening motive of the introduction returns, with a different rhythm, in the opening of section seven. Both Perry and Rossini use a dotted rhythm in the setting of versicle 13. The text (versicles 13 and 14) becomes more insistent, and the rhythmic activity is appropriately energetic in a faster tempo (allegro molto). Perry bases the vocal line with its wide leaps and dotted rhythms on the motive of the introduction of section one. At measure 190 a suggestion of the introductory motive recurs in the cellos in diminution (the melodic contour is the same).

The energy of movement subsides on the words *in planctu* ("in agony"). Here, to emphasize the text, Perry uses longer note values. No break occurs between sections seven and eight.

Section eight has a quiet character and is marked *misterioso* ("mysterious"). It is an appropriate setting for the text of these two versicles (15 and 16), which further entreats the Virgin Mary to help the poet share in the grief. A prominent improvisatory figure in the violins and a whole-tone melody in the vocal line reflect the mood. The half-step figure from the introduction (descending appoggiatura) recurs in the otherwise sustained accompaniment. A fermata (or pause) separates this section from section nine, which contains the longest introduction and the most rhythmic activity of all the divisions.

A whole-tone ostinato, a glissando, and the tempo (presto) create the feeling of improvisation, great activity, and anticipation in section nine. The whole-tone ostinato from d to d' lasts through most of the section. The text (versicles 17 and 18) expresses the desires and vehemence of the poet. Diminished fifths precede the entrance of the voice, similar to measures 15–17 in section one and and measures 44–46 in section two. The vocal material, with a recitative-like character, is more syncopated than that of previous sections, adding to the intensity. The motive of the introduction of section one returns, treated imitatively, with each line presenting a different accompaniment figure as the next entrance of the motive occurs. A two-part counterpoint doubled in octaves begins and creates a dissonant effect. The dotted rhythm as used here is also very prominent in Rossini's setting of versicles 16 and 17 (Ex. 35). Tremolos at measures 271–278 reinforce the text: *inflammatus et accensus* ("Here I stand inflam'd and excited") (versicle 18). This section ends with a slower rhythmic movement parallel quartal chords, and the descending appoggiatura motive from section one. Open fifths on B and F♯ against a dissonant F lead without pause to the final section.

Section ten (versicles 19 and 20) begins with a change of mood and tempo. This section has a slower and calmer character. A descending vocal line in a low tessitura (the general range of a

Ex. 35 *Stabat Mater.* Comparison of rhythms.

Ex. 36 Comparison of text settings of versicle 19.

melody or voice part) and tremolos in the lower strings depict the text speaking of death with the words *quando corpus morietur.* By comparison, Rossini's setting of the same text is very similar. He uses the bass voice with a descending melodic line as shown in Ex. 36. Perry repeats a portion of this descending line in the violin II part overlapping with a rising vocal line. The work ends with an intense quiet, as the vocal line rises against a sustained accompaniment while the dynamic level moves from a fortissimo to pianissimo. The vocal line again suggests the tonality of D at the end.

Besides its intensity and eloquence, Perry's *Stabat Mater* exhibits vestiges of improvisatory techniques in her probably unconscious recall and transformation of certain unrelated parts of Pergolesi's and Rossini's *Stabat Mater*. One cannot be sure, of course, but the irregularity and unpredictability of Perry's reference to some of the musical ideas of Pergolesi and Rossini reveal her intuitive, subconscious level of composition. To Julia Perry, music was an intense emotional experience. Her training provided her with several musical sources. She used the black idiom, traditional European practices, and twentieth century methods to create an eclectic style—her major contribution to the music of America.

Chapter Five

Evelyn Pittman
(1910-   )

Evelyn Pittman's deep interest in music as a child led her to a career as an educator, choral director, author, and composer. As early as the first grade, she could make up songs and earned a reputation as a prodigious story-teller.[1]

Evelyn LaRue Pittman was born January 6, 1910, in McAlester, Oklahoma. After her father's death, the family moved to Oklahoma City where she attended public schools. She completed her high school years at Highland Park in Detroit, Michigan, where she had moved to live with her older brother. Active in the school's musical organizations, she became the first black to sing in the school's well-known choir.

During the summer following graduation, Pittman returned to Oklahoma City. She trained a young adult choir from the Tabernacle Baptist Church to enter the district contest held for church choirs in that area. Under her direction the choir won the contest that year and each summer for the following three years.

Pittman's only sister, Blanche, was a graduate of Spelman College, a prestigious school for black women in Atlanta, Georgia. She encouraged Evelyn to attend the school and in 1929, Evelyn enrolled. There she studied with Kemper Harreld, renowned black violinist and head of the music departments at Spelman and Morehouse Colleges.

In the summer following her junior year, she enrolled in a black American history course at Atlanta University, which proved to be an awakening. She began to feel a "surge of new pride and a strong sense of belonging to a great race."[2] She discovered the omissions made by white historians in reporting the achievements of the black man in America and learned of her own great-uncle, Dred Winberly, who served two terms in the House of Representatives in North Carolina in 1879 and later served a term in the State Senate. A carpenter by trade, he was responsible for the reopening of the North Carolina University after the Civil War.[3] Pittman decided to commit herself to presenting black history through music.[4]

Pittman composed her first music at Spelman. During her senior year she wrote original music for a play produced by the Morehouse-Spelman Players. This work received honorable mention in *Crisis*, a magazine published by the NAACP. Following graduation in 1933 she entered Langston University in Langston, Oklahoma, to complete requirements for teaching certification in Oklahoma and received a life certificate in both public school music and history.

She began her teaching career in Oklahoma City at the Wheatly Junior High School. During her first year she organized and trained a thirty-piece orchestra and a forty-voice chorus, and presented an operetta. She also taught in the elementary grades. In a weekly radio program for the city school system, she demonstrated teaching techniques with her 100-voice chorus of fourth, fifth, and sixth graders. Many of the broadcasts were sent abroad as exchange material.

When her sister, who taught music in one of the elementary schools, wanted a song to teach her class about Frederick Douglass, Pittman wrote it. The class liked the song so much that she continued to write other songs about black leaders. Within six months she had written twenty one songs and short stories about famous black Americans. In 1944, with the advice of the late C. B. Macklin, former Oklahoma City music critic, she published *Rich Heritage*, a collection of these songs. She sent a copy of the book to Eleanor Roosevelt, who immediately sent a letter of congratulations.

Pittman founded a professional choir in 1938 that bore her name and for many years the Evelyn Pittman Choir performed in Oklahoma City and made local radio broadcasts. During one six month period NBC radio aired this weekly program, "Southern Rivers." The choir became philanthropic, gave music scholarships to Langston University, and made other donations to local charities. In its first year the choir represented Oklahoma and Texas at the Chicago World's Fair.[5] For the choir she arranged spirituals including *Rocka Mah Soul, Anyhow, Sit Down Servant,* and *Nobody Knows de Trouble I See.* Pittman also conducted a 300-voice interdenominational choir in concerts sponsored annually by the YWCA in Oklahoma City. These programs included such guest artists as Marian Anderson, William Warfield, Todd Duncan, and Etta Moten.

During this time she wrote a column, "Lady Evelyn Speaks," for an Oklahoma City newspaper, *The Black Dispatch.* Through her column she corresponded with soldiers during World War II.

In 1948 Pittman moved to New York City to attend the Juilliard School of Music where she studied composition with Robert Ward. While at Juilliard she wrote music for a stage work, *Again the River,* with story narration by Helen Schuyler.

When white universities lifted racial bars in the southern and border states, she decided to attend the University of Oklahoma in Norman and studied composition with Harrison Kerr, dean of the College of Fine Arts. Here she began her folk opera for an all-black cast, *Cousin Esther,* originally entitled *Esther and Cousin Mordecai* after the Biblical story. She was responsible for the libretto, music and orchestration, and operatic production. Kerr remembered later that she was influenced by George Gershwin's *Porgy and Bess,* "but not to the extent that she imitated the style."[6] She used the first scene of the work as a thesis for her master of music degree which she received from the university in 1954.

Kerr, a former student of Nadia Boulanger, wrote to Boulanger about the possibility of Pittman studying with her. In the summer of 1954 Pittman went to Paris for an interview with Boulanger. Boulanger listened to a first draft of Pittman's opera score and said, "I comprehend what you are doing, and it's charming, charming, charming. . . . Come back and let me help you. You have the spark."[7] In 1956 Pittman returned to France and began her studies. During her stay in Paris she completed *Cousin Esther* and had it performed there. She had excerpts of the opera presented at the American Church and for UNESCO in April, 1957. On May 7 and 10 of the same year the entire work was performed at the International Theater in Paris by an international cast of university students sponsored by the cultural centers of the American Embassy, Cité Universitaire, the American Church, and the American House. Edmond Pendleton conducted the orchestra for these performances.

After her return to the United States, she had excerpts from the opera presented in New York City at Carnegie Recital Hall, Manhattan's Colonial Park, and Woodlands High School in Hartsdale, New York. Radio station WNYC broadcast the work during its American Music Festival of 1963. *Cousin Esther* received outstanding reviews from both French and New York critics. One critic, Perdita Duncan of the *New York Amsterdam News*, said "It had the scope and pageantry of 'Aida.' "[8]

In 1958 Pittman moved to White Plains, New York, where she joined the music faculty at Woodlands High School in nearby Hartsdale. Her high school chorus sang at the World's Fair in New York in 1965, and had the distinction of being one of the few high school groups to perform with Duke Ellington's band. Aside from her creative pursuits and teaching, Pittman also found time to develop and train a choir at the Bethel Baptist Church in Westchester County, New York.

She had the second edition of her book, *Rich Heritage*, released in 1968. Since that time she has served as an educational consultant in workshops that demonstrate the uses of her book. Work on the second volume was interrupted by the tragic news of the assassination of Dr. Martin Luther King, Jr. His death shattered her. Pittman set aside work on the book and began to write a play based on the life of King because, as she later reflected, she "felt that King's memory should be kept alive." The play begins with the arrest of Rosa Parks in Montgomery, Alabama, in 1955 and King's rise as a civil rights leader. It traces his life to his assassination and ends with a 1970 birthday celebration for him.

The opera, *Freedom Child*, began to take shape when Pittman and her students at Woodlands High School were preparing a musical program for a neighboring school in New York. She decided to present a program on the life of King; so she set music to portions of the play. Following this performance, Pittman completed the work and presented a full production using students in 1970. In 1971 and 1972 the Woodlands Touring Choir performed this music drama in the northern and southeastern states and on a tour of the Scandinavian countries of Norway, Sweden, and Denmark. Several members of the King family attended the performance in Atlanta, Georgia. Rev. M. L. King, Sr. said "I have seen many productions based on the life of our son, Martin, but the one we have seen today, 'Freedom for Every Mother's Child,' is the most authentic."[9] The Woodlands ensemble and an Oklahoma cast have since performed the work in several other states and countries including England, Scotland, Italy, Liberia, and and Ghana.

In 1976 Pittman retired from her position at Woodlands High School and returned to Oklahoma City. Since then she has devoted herself to the Freedom Child Theater Group, a non-profit, charitable organization designed to promote better race relations through the presentation of musical dramas. In 1978 Pittman and the cast toured Europe performing *Freedom Child*, and she began working on her new opera, *Jim Noble*. It is a musical docu-drama about the life of the black man who transferred the state seal of Oklahoma from the originally selected capital city of Guthrie to Oklahoma City in 1910. Oklahoma City was to have become the capital by law, in 1913, and this musical highlights much of the shrewd political maneuvering that surrounded the event. Excerpts from this work already have enjoyed successful performances. It had one performance, sponsored by the Oklahoma Historical Society, given as part of "Blacks in the Westward Movement" presented in conjunction with the Black Heritage Week in Oklahoma City in February, 1979.

I Black History Through Music

Pittman's opportunity to realize her dream of teaching black history in music came in 1942 when she consented to write a song about statesman Frederick Douglass for a group of elementary music students. She continued composing other songs about outstanding blacks for the class and when she found she had completed enough songs and short biographies she decided to publish a book about distinguished black Americans and entitled it *Rich Heritage*.

Volume one of *Rich Heritage* contains short biographical

sketches and original songs about twenty-one black Americans. It is for unison singing with piano accompaniment for use at the elementary level, kindergarten through grade six. She published the first edition in 1944 and the second edition, with minor revisions, in 1968.

Volume two, now in preparation, will feature the contributions of additional Afro-Americans. This volume also will include rounds and two and three part songs as well as unison songs.

The outstanding personalities of volume one include black Americans from the past:

> Marian Anderson (Singer)
> Crispus Attucks (Soldier)
> Benjamin Banneker (Astronomer, Inventor, Mathematician)
> Harry T. Burleigh (Singer, Composer)
> George Washington Carver (Scientist)
> Frederick Douglass (Statesman)
> Paul Lawrence Dunbar (Poet)
> Todd Duncan (Singer, Actor)
> C. Rosenburg Foster (Trash Craft Queen)
> W. C. Handy ("Father of the Blues")
> Kemper Harreld (Violinist, Music Educator)
> Roland Hayes (Singer)
> Joe Louis (Boxing Champion)
> Inman Page (Oklahoma Educator)
> Paul Robeson (Singer, Actor, Athlete)
> Bill "Bojangles" Robinson (Dancer, Actor)
> Henry O. Tanner (Painter)
> Sojourner Truth (Race Leader)
> Booker T. Washington (Educator)
> Phillis Wheatley (Poetess)
> L. K. Williams (Minister)

The songs have melodies and rhythms suitable for young singers and are similar to material in many elementary music series. It provides variety of music learning experiences in music reading, simple musical design, and patterns of pitch and rhythms, and uses musical terms and signs.

Each song features a brief introduction for piano; the accompaniments are generally simple patterns with traditional chord progressions. The vocal line, in most cases, is duplicated in the accompaniment. Pittman uses both major and minor tonalities with a preference for the picardy (major) third at the end of the songs in minor keys.

The songs, with texts by the composer, are all in simple strophic settings and have rather limited ranges (usually within one octave). The melodic lines are basically very simple. There are some embellishments which imply improvisation (Ex. 37). Though much of the melodic movement is by step, certain intervallic movements provide material for teaching characteristics of tonal patterns such as high-low or movement by skips (Ex. 38). The same is true of many of the rhythmic patterns in the songs. (Ex. 39).

II Choral Works

Shortly after Pittman began her teaching career in Oklahoma City, she gained prominence as an effective, energetic, and capable conductor of choral and instrumental groups. Her experience in working with church choirs during her teenage years provided a rich background for her future work with choral organizations.

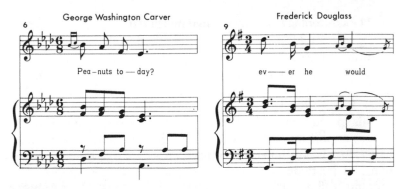

Ex. 37 *Rich Heritage.* Embellishments in vocal line.

Ex. 38 *Rich Heritage.* Intervallic movement and direction in vocal lines.

Ex. 39 *Rich Heritage.* Variety of rhythmic patterns.

Pittman arranged the spiritual melody *Anyhow,* a melody also known by the title *By 'n By,* for a cappella chorus of mixed voices. Carl Fischer, Inc. published it in 1952. Pittman dedicated it to her sister, Blanche P. Clardy.

This spiritual has a Verse-Refrain structure as shown in Fig. 12.

This arrangement is the shortest of the four spirituals analyzed here. There is only one verse and refrain, set off by a brief introduction and postlude. The style throughout is Call-Response. The sopranos call and the rest of the chorus responds. The composer

Fig. 12 Formal Outline of *Anyhow.*

Section	Introduction	Verse	Refrain	Postlude
No. of Meas.	2	8	8	2
Setting	Wordless Chorus	Sopranos sing melody (call) and altos, tenors and basses sing response		Wordless as in introduction except for word "Anyhow" at end of last phrase.
Dynamic	pp	Cres. <f> p <f <ff> mf> p		pp

adopted this style because the rhythmic ebb and flow of the melody lends itself to this type of setting. Once begun, the antiphonal pattern dominates throughout with the exception of the last phrase of the verse and refrain "cause I'm on my way to heaven anyhow." Here all the voices sing the phrase together.

The work is slow with a flowing quality and has an arch shape dynamically.

Pittman published *Sit Down, Servant,* arranged for mixed chorus with alto and baritone solos, with Carl Fischer, Inc. in 1949. The verses and refrains follow a symmetrical pattern as shown in Fig. 13.

The iambic rhythm of the first two words, "Sit down," dominates this spiritual. This syncopated rhythm appears in the first phrase at the beginning and end as follows:

Sit down, servant,   can't sit down

In the first measure, the "sit down" motive syncopates the first and second beats while in the second measure it syncopates the second and third beats. This alternation of position in the measure gives the spiritual its sprightly vitality that belies the words "sit down." The music constantly springs up.

Fig. 13 Over-all form of *Sit Down, Servant.*

Section	Refrain	Verse 1	Verse 2	Refrain	Verse 3	Verse 4	Refrain
No. of Meas.	8	8	8	10	8	8	10
Medium	Chorus	Alto solo and wordless Chorus	Baritone solo and wordless Chorus	Chorus	Alto solo and wordless Chorus	Baritone solo and wordless Chorus	Chorus
Key	f minor			→	c minor		→

Fig. 14 Form of *Nobody Knows de Trouble I See.*

Section	Introduction	Refrain	Verse 1	Varied Refrain	Verse 2	Shortened (varied intro.) Refrain
No. of Meas.	6	8	8	8	8	5

Pittman wisely makes the rhythmic vitality of this melody the center of attention. The harmony is quite direct. The bass has an independent part in the refrains, but it complements the word rhythm of the soprano, alto, and tenor. In the verses, the chorus provides a wordless background consisting of sustained chords to set off the moving solos to best advantage.

She had *Nobody Knows de Trouble I See* published in 1954 by Carl Fischer, Inc. It is for a cappella chorus of mixed voices with an unspecified solo voice written in the treble clef.

She uses divided vocal parts, four to seven parts, at various points. The work has a Verse-Refrain structure as shown in Fig. 14.

The rhythmic character of this song is syncopated, but its text is a lament, not a portrait of restless energy. The melody is entirely diatonic, but the harmony is quite chromatic, especially in the introduction and verse sections. She chose, perhaps unconsciously, to use chromatic harmony in the style of famous laments like the "Lament" from *Dido and Aeneas* by Purcell and the "Crucifixus" from Bach's *B Minor Mass*. However there is no ground bass (a short melody that is repeated over and over in the lowest voice). Ex. 40 shows the chromatically altered chords used in *Nobody Knows de Trouble I See* which contain tones outside of the key of G major (E♭, B♭, E♯, F♮, and A♭). In fact, chromatically altered or not, the accompanying voices move more independently and freely than in any other spiritual arrangement analyzed in this study.

The texture of this work constantly shifts from homophony to polyphony. For example, the introduction is basically a homophonic section for four-part, men's chorus until the final phrase when the women's voices, in three parts, join with the spiritual melody against the men's voices. In the varied refrain more polyphonic treatment occurs where the chorus accompanies the solo melody with different ostinato-like patterns. The choral parts use two basic rhythmic patterns: one in the soprano I and bass voices, ⁴₄ 𝅗𝅥 𝅗𝅥 and the other in the soprano II, alto, and tenor voices. ⁴₄ ♪ ♪ ♪ ♪ ♪ ♪ ♪ ♪.

Pittman's arrangement of *Rocka Mah Soul*, published in 1952 by Carl Fischer, Inc., was dedicated to her mother, Mrs. Florence K. Greer.

This work demonstrates a blending of the black communal experience of spiritual singing with the white American tradition of strict choral discipline. The a cappella performance and Refrain-

Ex. 40 *Nobody Knows de Trouble I see.* Meas. 1-2, 19-20, chromatically altered chords.

Verse from the original spiritual is faithfully preserved. The solo baritone singing with the chorus suggests a minister or song leader drawing choral responses from a congregation. In the final two phrases of the refrain, the baritone soloist and the first sopranos of the chorus sing a rather free heterophonic duet (a slightly modified version of the same melody by two singers) in improvisatory style against the rhythmic chanting of the chorus. These three remnants of original spiritual performance practices add authenticity to the arrangement.

However, the precisely notated rhythms with carefully synchronized syncopations demand a very precise, well-rehearsed performance, typical of professional choruses in the United States. In addition, Pittman writes sharp contrasts of range; precise, carefully articulated rhythms tied to the rhythm of the words; and an intricate passing of the melody back and forth between the second sopranos and altos. One would not hear a precise, polished setting like this in the original, unrehearsed group of black worshipers who had assembled simply to express their religious feelings spontaneously.

The setting seems to be for a five-part chorus and baritone solo, but in reality the basic chorus only consists of four voices; soprano, alto, tenor, and bass. Pittman divides the sopranos of the choir into first and second in order to use some of the sopranos to sing with the chorus and a smaller number to provide vocal embellishment in a high register contrasting to the low register of the solo baritone. The first soprano part is actually a rather freely roving part. It sometimes doubles the second sopranos at irregular intervals as in the first refrain; sometimes it is a heterophonic part an octave higher as in the second and third refrains; or it has sustained pedal tones as in the second verse.

The role of the baritone soloist is also both melodic and embellishing. He doubles the melody an octave lower than the second sopranos and altos in the first two verses and refrains, and, in the final two statements of the refrain, sings an embellishing part that is heterophonic to the first sopranos as indicated in the figure below. The heterophonic treatment used in the last refrain appears in Ex. 41.

The piece begins rather quietly and unfolds gradually, finally culminating in the last refrain with the first sopranos and solo

Fig. 15 Formal Outline of *Rocka Mah Soul.*

	Refrain		Verse 1	Refrain	Verse 2		Refrain	
No. of Meas.	8	8	8	8	8	8	8	8 + 8
Medium	Chorus	Chorus; Baritone soloist	Chorus; Baritone soloist	Chorus	Chorus; Baritone soloist	Chorus	Chorus; Baritone soloist	

Ex. 41 *Rocka Mah Soul.* Meas. 56-59, the heterophonic treatment in last refrain.

baritone singing improvised embellishment of the melody in the chorus. Unlike many passages of notated music that try unsuccessfully to capture the spontaneous sound of improvisation, this written, improvisatory passage sounds natural. The arrangement proves effective in performances by non-black choirs to whom the spontaneous, congregational performance of spirituals is foreign.

Simply by reading the work as the arranger has notated it, any choral group of sufficient skill can capture the improvisation.

Pittman's works, especially her operas, show her instinctive dramatic sense. She uses the black idiom in much of her writing and draws upon the music of the black church. Her published works include music for the elementary grades, solo vocal works, and spiritual arrangements for mixed chorus. She continues today to compose works to promote and preserve the history of black Americans.

Chapter Six

Lena McLin
(1929-   )

Lena Johnson McLin inherited a rich musical legacy from her mother's family. Her uncle is Thomas A. Dorsey, the blues singer "Georgia Tom" and "Father of Gospel Music." The Dorseys had immersed themselves in music and McLin's mother continued the family tradition.

McLin was born in Atlanta, Georgia, on September 5, 1929. Her father was minister of the Greater Mt. Calvary Baptist Church in Atlanta, and her mother was the church's music teacher and choir director. McLin's mother was deeply religious and believed in strict discipline in the rearing of children. She provided McLin's early training with piano lessons and exposure to many types of music. She often took her to concerts and operas, and played recordings of symphonies and other serious music. McLin's interest in the piano was evident at this time. She later said that her mother's strict attention to her early music education helped to build her "ear and musical sense."[1]

Because her father and mother were minister and choir director, McLin attended church services at least three times each Sunday. Her mother had a rare spontaneous creative talent and composed and arranged songs for the church choir. As a teenager McLin tried to emulate her mother and wrote and performed short piano pieces to which she gave such imposing titles as "Sonata Opus 10, No. 1." McLin says that these sonatas constitute the beginning of her compositional career. During this time she assisted her mother in the teaching and directing of the church choir. She taught the anthems, which were considered "classical music," while her mother taught the gospel music.

Another important early influence on McLin was her grand-mother, who had been born a slave. She introduced her to her familial and racial heritage by singing many of the older spirituals. She later remembered these melodies as she searched for folk material for her choral arrangements.

McLin attended the public schools of Atlanta but also spent several years during her youth in Chicago. She went to Chicago to live intermittently with her uncle, Thomas A. Dorsey, who had composed *Precious Lord, Take My Hand* and *There Will be Peace in the Valley* among others. While she absorbed her uncle's music, on the conscious level she preferred classical music and spirituals over the blues and gospel styles.

Her uncle was the oldest of seven children, all of whom played piano, guitar or banjo, and sang. All the brothers and sisters were also talented in composing and arranging music but only her uncle pursued a career as composer. He had switched from blues to gospel music in the 1920s. At this time both the blues and gospel music were considered of little use to the student of serious music, which may account for McLin's musical tastes and her later denial that this music had influenced her. However, the careful listener to her music can detect turns of phrase and harmony that show her unconscious assimilation of her uncle's style.

After graduation from high school, she enrolled in Spelman College in Atlanta, the same college attended by Evelyn Pittman. Her choice of music as a major was automatic, but she found obstacles. A serious hand operation at this time threatened to end her plans for a career as a pianist. Through her own strong will to succeed and a sympathetic teacher, Florence Brinkman Boyton, she eventually played many difficult works, such as Rachmaninoff's *Second Piano Concerto*, that once had seemed impossible. McLin also studied violin at Spelman and was a student of Leonora Brown and Willis Lawrence James in music theory and composition.

After she received her bachelor's degree, she moved to Chicago. She married and became the mother of two children. With custom-ary thoroughness, McLin turned her interest to courses in child psychology and general education. Later she enrolled in music courses at Roosevelt University. Her studies included electronic music. She also studied voice with Thelma Waide Brown, a black singer and vocal teacher who was a contemporary of Marian Anderson.

McLin became a functional composer. She directed church choirs for many years and wrote an anthem, call, and hymn (words and music) for each Sunday during one seven-year period. She wrote them to fit the text of the sermons. The medium of each work varied to fit the voices in the choir that Sunday.[2]

The influence of the black church and its music is evident in McLin's musical style. Characteristics of the gospel style, for example, appear in many of her works: segmented passages, implied improvisation, repetition of short phrases, and embellishments of the vocal and instrumental melodic lines. Examples occur in *Eucharist of the Soul* (a liturgical mass for the Episcopal service), *Sanctus and Benedictus, We Just Got to Have Peace All Over This World, Free At Last* (a cantata), and *If They Ask You Why He Came* (a gospel song).

McLin deplores the rejection of gospel music by so many serious musicians:

> I know that some of us avoid the gospel, thinking it makes us look small. This is the same thing the spiritual went through, but it managed to survive the disdain and disrespect of the second generation. . . . I think, too, that the day has come when we ought to stop being ashamed of any folk contribution![3]

She sees an importance in distinguishing between the spiritual and the gospel song. "A spiritual," she says, "is a folk song, originated by the black American, which must have a personal relationship with deity. . . . It's been handed down from generation to generation. . . . Gospel songs are composed, but the singer expresses this music in a personal style, free, unrestricted in any way."[4] Concerning the status of gospel music, she says:

> From 1924, the hidden folk idiom has been the gospel song and it has had a forceful denial by the elite and structured musician. In every race the creative people have to draw from

the folk, and they (creative people) have to chart the way we are to go. The structured musician is the 'philosopher' of music—he must put it down and preserve it (folk contribution). The folk never preserve—they always put it in the raw. It is there, but the serious musicians have to take it and make it into something. That is why I feel that there will be an emphasis by at least some of the structured musicians to deal with the gospel song in the proper manner.[5]

The musical impact of the gospel song, according to McLin, "depends on the ability of the singer to interpret, to 'worry' the notes. It can't be sung straight. That's not living the experience."[6] When McLin writes in the gospel style, she says that her aim is to place emphasis on the accompaniment with enough written improvisation to compensate for performers who lack the ability to worry the notes. It is her goal to write gospel songs that demand correct vocal technique.

McLin does not limit her style to the use of gospel characteristics. Her works show a variety of influences such as the liberated dissonances found in *The Torch Has Been Passed, The Earth is the Lord's, Let the People Sing Praise Unto the Lord,* and *Free At Last,* as well as rock styles in her *In This World* (a collection of SATB choruses) and *If We Could Exchange Places.* Additional characteristics of her choral works include frequent use of natural word rhythms, syncopated rhythms, imitation, and unison writing. Often, she contrasts the choral sonority with an independent instrumental accompaniment.

In 1969 McLin became head of the music department at Kenwood High School in Chicago. She has attained outstanding success as a composer-arranger, clinician, and educator working with inner-city students. She received the honor of being named leading black choral composer by the National Association of Negro Musicians (NANM) in 1970; outstanding composer by the Critics Association in 1971; and teacher of the year in Chicago in 1972. She received both the Outstanding Composer Award in 1973 and an honorary degree in 1975 from Virginia Union University.

McLin played an important role in the establishment of the music major curriculum for the Chicago Public Schools; her school was one of the three in Chicago that hosted the pilot music major program. Several years ago McLin served as an advisor on the unit on rock for the MENC (Music Educators National Conference).

McLin believes that teachers must understand the meanings of the lyrics in the songs of today. Her interest lies in youth and the rock movement; she feels obligated to avoid what she calls the "amoral" songs of the 60s and 70s.[7] She has written her own topical texts such as *We Just Got to Have Peace All Over This World*, *If We Could Exchange Places*, *I'm Moving Up*, *Miracle For Me*, and *In This World*. These songs, she says, present a positive view for youths. She has also arranged many songs for vocal groups singing in night clubs, theaters, or colleges.

McLin has conducted workshops at various colleges and universities in many states including Florida, Illinois, Indiana, Iowa, Maryland, Massachusetts, New Jersey, New York, and Tennessee. Her courses include traditional teaching methods, black music, and related performance practices. She has often served as clinician at divisional and national MENC meetings.

In the early 1960s she founded the McLin Opera Company to provide an outlet for professional singers in Chicago who were unable to obtain this experience elsewhere and to produce operatic works, a variety of stage works, and concerts.

McLin has written a textbook, *Pulse—A History of Music*, published by Neil A. Kjos Music Company in 1977. Designed for high school music survey courses, it includes American music, European music, popular music, and black music and musicians.

McLin's compositions include cantatas, masses, spirituals (solo and choral arrangements), works in spiritual styles and gospel styles, anthems, art songs, "art-rock" songs, operas (for kindergarten through high school levels—including "rock" operas), soul songs, works for piano, orchestral works, and electronic music. Her music has received performances both in the United States and abroad.

In the early 1960s McLin, impressed by John F. Kennedy and the New Frontier, selected Kennedy's inaugural speech as the basis for the text of *The Torch Has Been Passed*. The text is a pronouncement of peace—"We shall have no war. . . . This is the new generation of love."

This work, published by General Words and Music Company in

1971, contains syncopated rhythms, unison passages, an ostinato pattern, and dissonant passages. The form is ternary with an introduction and coda as illustrated in the figure below.

The introduction begins with unison chorus for two measures. The remainder of the introduction is for four-part chorus with prominent use of word rhythms and syncopated rhythmic patterns on the word "Americans." The A section presents the text, "We shall have no war" in a syncopated rhythmic pattern which occurs frequently.

We shall have no   war.

A two-part ostinato pattern begins section B with the women's voices in unison against the men's voices in unison and in contrary motion. A few selected voices, in three-part harmony, sing a rhythmic chant-like figure above the ostinato. The section ends with three measures of the ostinato alone. The A' section combines the A material and the chant-like figure (selected voices) of section B, in both unison and three-part writing. The selected voices drop out. She varies the choral material and extends it through repetition, providing a coda to end the work.

I   Sacred Works

McLin's career as composer of choral music actually began with her compositions for the church choirs. Her anthem, *Let the People Sing Praise Unto the Lord*, expresses her theological beliefs. Published in 1973 by General Words and Music Company, it is for

Fig. 16 Form of *The Torch Has Been Passed.*

	Introduction	A	B	A'	Coda
No. of Meas.	6	16	27	16	7

mixed chorus with keyboard (piano or organ) and B♭ trumpet accompaniment.

The work includes driving rhythms, syncopated patterns, and quartal and mildly dissonant harmonies. The form of the work is ternary with an introduction and coda.

The introduction is for solo trumpet and keyboard accompaniment. The trumpet solo plays in a fanfare style and features a prominent triplet figure on a single tone (E). The keyboard part uses quartal chords providing an accompaniment for the rather disjunct line of the solo. A slight ritard and crescendo (to fff) lead to section A for chorus and keyboard accompaniment. Each phrase of the choral part features syncopated rhythms. The choir sings "Alleluia" three times, each time with the same rhythm, but with change in pitch at the end of each phrase.

Section B also has quartal harmonies. The section features the instruments with choral interjections. Both instruments (trumpet and keyboard) have material based on the "Alleluia" phrases taken from the A section.

A literal repeat of section A follows. The coda begins with the first phrase from section A. Immediately following is a short a cappella section for chorus with the varied and extended material of section A. The work ends with four measures of alternation between instruments and chorus, a literal repeat of the last four measures of section B.

II The Gospel Style

McLin's works represent a variety of compositional styles: the Baroque chorale style, contemporary dissonant styles, modern popular and rock styles, and traditional gospel styles. This diversity

Fig. 17 Form of *Let The People Sing Praise Unto the Lord.*

	Introduction	A	B	A	Coda (A')
No. of Meas.	8	8	20	8	14

reflects her training in the European techniques and exposure to the music of black Americans, especially the music of her uncle Thomas A. Dorsey.

McLin has published several gospel songs for mixed chorus. She dedicated *If They Ask You Why He Came*, published in 1971 by General Words and Music Company, to her brother, Rev. B. J. Johnson, III. It is for accompanied mixed chorus with text by McLin, and the form is binary with an introduction and coda (Fig. 18).

The introduction begins with a secondary dominant-seventh chord, and the progression, which has more secondary dominant-seventh chords, avoids the tonic until the end of the section, finally establishing the tonality. This is the harmonic treatment in nearly all of the phrases of the piece. At the end of the first phrase of the introduction the melody has embellishments which suggest an improvisatory style. The entire introduction is wordless; the voices sing the syllable "Oo."

Section A has a slightly faster tempo than the introduction. The left hand of the accompaniment has typical rhythmic patterns found in contemporary gospel performances (Ex. 42).

The chorus sings a more expressive part against the accompaniment rhythms and repeats the entire section.

Section B, also repeated, presents other gospel performance styles. The accompaniment features a rapid triplet figure in the left hand in several measures to accompany sustained chords in the vocal parts (Ex. 43). The embellishments of the right hand of the accompaniment and the soprano line are other examples of gospel style characteristics in this piece.

Fig. 18 Form of *If They Ask You Why He Came* ‖: and :‖ mean repeat).

	Introduction	A		B		B extended	Coda
		‖:	:‖	‖:	:‖		
No. of Meas.	6	16		19		8	6

Ex. 42 *If They Ask You Why He Came.* Meas. 7-8, accompaniment rhythmic pattern of left hand.

Ex. 43 *If They Ask You Why He Came.* Meas. 27, triplet figure in left hand of accompaniment.

The coda is an almost literal repeat of the introduction. The final phrase ending is basically the same with octave displacement.

In gospel accompaniments, the scores simply serve as an outline to which the performer adds improvisations. Here McLin has written the accompaniment with embellishments and other implied improvisational effects normally left to the performer, but with provisions for other desired improvisation.

II   A Portrait of Martin Luther King, Jr.

McLin subtitled her cantata *Free At Last,* "A Portrait of Martin Luther King, Jr." In traditional terms it is a passion cantata, a setting of the story of the death of Christ as told in one of the four gospels. Here the drama centers on the role of Martin Luther King in freeing blacks in America and his death. The work does not attempt to immortalize him in pretentious poetry and music. Rather, it is a contemporary recreation of the black experience of an unceasing, often bitter struggle for freedom and equality. The themes of violence and repression dominate the work. Slaves are repressed, forbidden an education, and beaten. Then, after emancipation, they are repressed politically and socially.

In presenting recent history, the cantata depicts how blacks experience the protest rallies. Marchers go to jail, listen to sermons, and sing gospel songs, marching songs, and spirituals. They suffer, struggle, and exult in their success under King.

The text, written by McLin, is terse and repetitive like a spiritual. She conceived the music and text together as a unit for the strongest impact upon the listener, an impact heightened by the recognizable spiritual. In regard to idiom, it does not resemble a traditional work like a Bach cantata or Handel oratorio.

Five spiritual melodies appear in the course of the work—"Sometimes I Feel Like a Motherless Child," "Mama, is Massa Gonna Sell Us Tomorrow," "Can't You Hear those Freedom Bells Ringing," "He Had to Move When the Spirit Say Move," and "Free At Last"—all of these express the black experience in America. The conventional, Christian and Judaic personages—Jesus Christ, Moses, Joshua, and others—are absent. Abraham Lincoln is the only person mentioned by name. The chorus represents the people. King, as a leader of the freedom marches, appears as the baritone soloist in Section IV. Marching songs in the folk idiom invoke the freedom movement of the 1960s, and descriptive passages depict slave auctions and racial tension. One section near the end is in the style of a melodrama (instrumental accompaniment with a spoken text), a nineteenth century European form used by Beethoven in *Fidelio* and Schönberg in the *Gürrelieder*.

The cantata is in one continuous movement with pauses between sections, but no separation into large independent movements as in, for example, a conventional Lutheran cantata. It moves with great urgency. The rapidly changing musical scenery fuses into six scenes as follows:

  I. Introduction—"Sometimes I Feel Like A Motherless Child"
 II. Sold Into Slavery
III. Repression as Slaves—Emancipation—Repression as Free Men
 IV. Social Protest and Racial Conflict
  V. Climax of Racial Conflict—Death of King
 VI. Finale—*Free At Last*

McLin based the introduction almost entirely on the well-known spiritual "Sometimes I Feel Like a Motherless Child." The dramatic force derives from the gradual emergence of the spiritual during the section. We do not hear it in its complete form until the end when the soprano sings it simply, accompanied by the piano. Before this, we hear separate phrases, "Oh Freedom," ("True Believer" phrase) at the beginning and, later, "A long ways from home." The phrase, "A long ways from home," continues to be heard in the next section as a refrain.

The second section is entirely about slavery. She composed most of it in a contrapuntal idiom common to white Europeans but foreign to blacks. The principal idea, which recurs three times throughout the section, is a two-part canon on the text, "Slaves were taken and stood on blocks." This setting depicts the strangeness and hostility that Africans felt in being uprooted from their native countries, and sold into slavery in a foreign nation. Later in the cantata, McLin portrays hostility and conflict through dissonance and polytonality, but here she achieves it by means of idiom alone. She introduces one slave song, "Mama, is Massa gonna sell us tomorrow?", lending an authenticity to the section.

The third section centers on repression. A short passage in the middle addresses emancipation, but the music and text indicate that manumission, humane and well-meaning in itself, did little to improve the social relationships between blacks and whites. Word painting is prominent in this section. The harsh commands of the text, "Don't think! Don't Read!" leap in fortissimo, staccato chords alternated in piano and chorus. The effect resembles the mid-section of Handel's aria "He was despised" from the *Messiah* and "He smote the first-born of Egypt" from *Israel in Egypt*, but it does not develop; it flashes by in a few seconds. This motive returns briefly after emancipation on the words, "Beat Them, Lynch Them!", showing that political emancipation scarcely affected the social attitudes.

The middle of this section depicts emancipation in one strophe of the spiritual "Can't you hear those freedom bells ringing," a short chorale setting of the text "Lincoln signed the paper," and a reprise of the opening section of the introduction, "Oh Freedom." The composer weaves into the musical texture of this passage several melodies associated with freedom, which will be described later. The wealth of detail strengthens the dramatic impact. At the end of this section, oppression returns in the form of hooded men.

Although never mentioned by name, Martin Luther King appears in the fourth section which begins, "God sent a leader to right the nation's wrong." As in the other sections, spirituals are incorporated ("He Had to Move When the Spirit Say Move"), but a marching song written by the composer in folk style dominates the whole. A quotation of the text (but not the tune) of a famous protest song, "We Shall Not Be Moved," also appears in this section.[8] The form of the songs is strophic, like a folk song. The musical structure gives an interesting lesson in improvisation. McLin states the principal musical ideas at the beginning on the words "Jails could not hold him, liberty enfolds him" and "He came to Alabama, one strong to right a wrong." These two short phrases form the principal melodic material of the entire section which unfolds in a march-like idiom with two episodes depicting prayer and racial conflict and concluding with a spiritual, "He Had to Move When the Spirit Say Move."

The penultimate section is sermon-like with a narrator who addresses himself directly to God throughout. Background music is provided by the piano. Then the choir sings a capella. While the music recalls the protest songs and spirituals of the previous sections, the narrator reflects on the sufferings of the marchers, their physical exhaustion, and unjust accusations. Then the work turns to the Memphis Sanitation Workers' strike: "It happened on a day, a bright and sunny day, with singing birds and waving hands and dedication." The music does not weep, or even mention the death of King. Instead, we hear the spiritual "Can't You Hear Those Freedom Bells Ringing."

IV   Musical Style

The most remarkable feature of the entire work is the melodic invention. Most of the work is in the style of a folk song, a recitative, or a chorale melody. The melodies of five spirituals lend authenticity. Some appear in their entirety and others in part.

Occasionally, motives from several related spirituals cluster together, enriching musical associations. Such an instance occurs at
the beginning of the cantata with the simple words "Oh freedom,"
as illustrated in Ex. 44.

This beginning arouses many associations. The melody in measures 2–3 comes from a transitional phrase of "Sometimes I Feel Like
a Motherless Child" where the text is "True Believer," or, as sung
by Paul Robeson, "Come my brother" and "Come my sister" (Ex.
45).

The second two-measure melody in Ex. 44 exhibits a relationship
with two other freedom songs, "Oh Freedom" and a song called
simply "Freedom" as sung by Sidney Poitier to the tune of "Amen"
in the film *Lilies of the Field*. Both of the latter tunes begin with a
rising motive in a dotted half-quarter note rhythm (Ex. 46 and 47).
The contours of the entire melodies resemble the rise and fall of the
motive from measures 4–5 of Ex. 44, and, of course, they share a
common text. Later in the second section, the "Oh freedom" motive
(Ex. 46, meas. 1–2) appears as a contrast motive in the midst of text
and music about the brutalizing treatment of slaves as illustrated in
Ex. 48.

McLin exhibits an improvisatory background. In the fourth

Ex. 44 *Free At Last.* Meas. 2–5, opening motive.

Ex. 45 "True Believer" from "Sometimes I Feel Like a Motherless
Child."

Oh ———— free-dom   Oh ———— free—dom.

Ex. 46 "Oh Freedom."

Free ————— dom,   Free —— dom,   Free —— dom

Ex. 47 "Freedom."

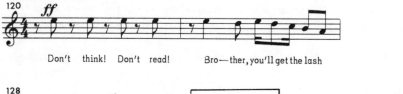

Andante molto
120 *ff*

Don't think! Don't read!   Bro—ther, you'll get the lash

128

Cry out! Oh free-dom!   Cry out! Oh free-dom!   Grant us thy s ooth—ing bo—— som,

Ex. 48 *Free At Last.* Section 2, meas. 120-121; 128-131, the "Oh freedom" motive as a contrast motive.

section on social protest and racial conflict, she states two principal melodic subjects in two four-measure phrases in hymn style, Ex. 49, and then fashions two marching songs from them in folk style for baritone solo.

Both phrases are in f natural minor. The first is the most repetitive, rhythmically and melodically. She uses it later with additional material. The second phrase contains a triplet figure in measure 202. This syncopated motive emphasizing the last beat of the measure

Ex. 49 *Free At Last.* Section 4, meas. 197-205, principal melody in hymn style.

furnished the basis of the first marching song of the section as illustrated in Ex. 50.

The melody of the marching song resembles the subject-answer of a fugue more than the usual folk song. The principal melody of four measures unfolds in d minor, and then repeats a fifth higher in the second four measures like the tonal answer of a fugue subject. The theme has the compact sound of a fugue subject. The texture is homophonic, however.

The second marching song begins with the words of a famous protest song, "We Shall Not Be Moved," but with new music (Ex.

Ex. 50 *Free At Last.* Section 4, meas. 208-216, first marching song.

Ex. 51 *Free At Last.* Section 4, meas. 257-264, second marching song.

Ex. 52 "I Shall Not Be Moved," beginning (original tune).

51). The original tune of "I Shall Not Be Moved" appears for comparison (Ex. 52).

Word painting enhances the original tune in the third and fourth measures. On the words "I shall not be moved," we hear a single note emphatically reiterated. The composed tune in Ex. 51 also emphasizes repeated notes, but the melodic contour differs from the original. Here the composer borrowed a phrase of the text and the pictorial idea of the song but not the melody itself. To this new melody she adds the contrasting phrase "Jails cannot hold us, Liberty enfolds us" taken from the introductory hymn illustrated in Ex. 49. Thus, the second marching song follows different structural principles than the first one. These tunes are essentially simple, outlining triads or simple intervals like the third or fifth. McLin preserves the innate simplicity of the folk song but avoids mere repetition.

Homophony is the basic texture of this piece. There is usually a leading melody with chordal or ostinato accompaniment. Here the chordal accompaniments differ considerably in style, depending on context. Near the beginning, McLin harmonizes the simple diatonic melody of "long ways from home" with a combination of chromatic and diatonic chords which pictorially represent the text. A distant progression from the central tonality of a minor is shown in Ex. 53, illustrating "long ways." At this point the progression reminds one of late nineteenth century German practice. On the word "home," however, the harmony immediately simplifies, moving to the tonic through a minor dominant chord. In this short passage we move from a highly chromatic style emphasizing leading tones to a modal diatonic progression avoiding them.

This harmonic style is basically triadic as is much of the work. However, a few harshly dissonant passages using quartal harmonies depict racial conflict, as in Ex. 54.

The baritone soloist sings a simple reciting tone style while the piano provides pictorial effects. The essential harmony in this passage is a quartal chord D-G-C in the right hand with minor seconds and major sevenths added ($G^\sharp$, $F^\sharp$, $D^\sharp$, and $C^\sharp$) primarily in the left hand. Throughout the section, the $G^\natural$ in the right hand clashes with the $G^\sharp$ in the left hand.

Other interesting harmonic effects include the blues harmoniza-

Ex. 53 *Free At Last.* Section 1, meas. 8-10, the highly chromatic progression used to pictorially represent the text.

tion of the hymn-like tune that introduces section 4 (See Ex. 49). In measure 204 of this example, McLin harmonizes the A♭ of the augmented triplet rhythmic motive as a dominant thirteenth in f minor moving immediately to a major tonic. One does not expect a *Tierce de Picardie* (picardy third) after a chord of this nature.

Finally, interesting examples of contrapuntal texture exist. Such departures occur because of the text. Near the beginning of section two, McLin writes a two-voice canon for the text, "Slaves were taken and stood on blocks in most parts of the new land." Empty intervals such as the fifth, octave, eleventh, and twelfth predominate (Ex. 55).

Note the wide separation between the parts and their pentatonic mode (five tone scale). It represents the slaves being separated from Africa and carried to a foreign country. It returns periodically throughout the second section.

Then, at the end of the fourth section, we hear another unusual contrapuntal device in this context, the *quodlibet* (different melodies or portions of melodies used simultaneously in different voices in a polyphonic setting). The spiritual tune "He Had to Go Where the Spirit Say Go" in $\frac{2}{4}$ combines with "America" in $\frac{3}{4}$ as illustrated in Ex. 56. This device also has a pictorial derivation. In his speech at

Ex. 54 *Free At Last.* Section 4, meas. 244-247, dissonant passage using quartal harmonies to depict racial conflict.

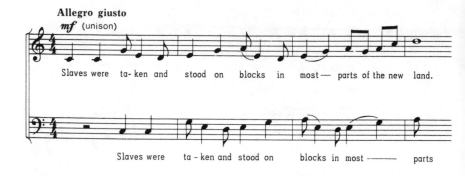

Ex. 55 *Free At Last.* Section 2, meas. 36-39, two-voice canon.

the march on Washington in 1963, King remarked that with the achievement of the reforms he advocated, voter rights, desegregation, and equal opportunities, he could proudly say "My country 'tis of thee." McLin combines the spiritual and the traditional patriotic hymn of America as symbolic of the difficulties in the integration of the two races.

Fig. 19 compares all six sections of *Free At Last* by tempo, medium, and key.

As discussed here, McLin's style covers a wide range of influences: traditional European techniques, twentieth century styles, and the folk and popular music of the black American. In her work she continues to experiment with the synthesis of black and European musics in new media.

Ex. 56 *Free At Last.* Section 4, meas. 313-321, *quodlibet.*

Fig. 19 Outline of *Free At Last*.

Scene (No. of meas.)	Tempo	Medium	Key
I. Introduction (meas. 1-10)	Freely	Chorus Sopranos	a minor
(meas. 11-33)	Slow and Sustained	Soprano solo and SATB Chorus	
II. Sold into Slavery (meas. 33-119)	Allegro giusto	Two part Chorus and SATB Chorus	C major A major a minor
III. Repression as Slaves (meas. 120-133)	Andante mosso	SATB Chorus	a minor
Emancipation (meas. 134-170)	Lively— Andante	SATB Chorus Soprano Solo	f minor
Repression as Free Men (meas. 171-192)	Presto— Andante	SATB Chorus	a minor
IV. Social Protest and Racial Conflict (meas. 193-205)	Andante Religioso	SATB Chorus	f minor
(meas. 206-304)	Alla Marcia and Changing Tempos	Baritone or Mezzosoprano Solo	d minor e minor d minor
(meas. 305-329)	Changing Tempos		c minor f minor
V. Climax of Racial Conflict (meas. 330-383)	Lento triste	Narrator and SATB Chorus	f minor
Death of King (meas. 384-409)	Andante pesante	SATB Chorus	f minor
VI. Finale—Free at Last (meas. 410-424)	Molto maestoso	SATB Chorus	F major

Chapter Seven

A Common Bond

These five black American women composers demonstrate a musical inventiveness. Their racial heritage and their contact with European music traditions combine the spontaneous creating of music with the tradition of written composition. We see the influence of folk, blues, jazz, rock, and gospel styles in the music of Florence Price, Margaret Bonds, Julia Perry, Evelyn Pittman, and Lena McLin.

Pervading the styles of each composer is the incorporation of the black folk idiom. Each composer has written several spiritual arrangements. They also have cultivated styles in their original works which are reminiscent of folk styles such as the spiritual and blues. The folk idiom is especially prominent in Bonds's *The Ballad of the Brown King* and *The Negro Speaks of Rivers*, and McLin's *Free At Last*.

The settings for the spiritual arrangements vary. Price's arrangements are, for the most part, direct and relatively simple. One exception, however, is her well-known arrangement of *My Soul's Been Anchored in de Lord* which features a very rhythmic setting marked by complex chromatic harmonies.

Bonds's jazz and blues influences are quite evident in her spiritual arrangements. The settings are dramatic with supportive accompaniments that complement the melodies. Her sometimes unusual accompaniments include jazz rhythms and chords.

Pittman prefers simplicity in choral settings. Her arrangements are especially unusual because she combines the black communal experience of spiritual singing with strict choral discipline and traditional harmonies. Perry's spiritual settings retain the purity and original character of the true folk style through uncomplicated accompaniments.

McLin's spiritual arrangements vary, ranging from chorale-like settings to quasi-folk style. In her cantata, *Free At Last*, one interesting example occurs near the beginning, where the composer harmonizes the simple diatonic melody of "long ways from home" with a combination of chromatic and diatonic chords to represent the text pictorially. The progression begins a distance from the central tonality. In general, however, McLin uses traditional chordal accompaniments for the spiritual melodies.

These five composers did not limit their works to a religious or folk style or to one performance medium. Their compositions range from orchestral works (Price's four symphonies and concerti; Julia Perry's *Stabat Mater* for solo voice and string quartet or orchestra) to chamber works, operas (Pittman, Perry, and McLin have had several operas performed), art songs, choral works, and keyboard compositions.

All of the composers were music educators. This role influenced the compositions of both Pittman and McLin; each created for teaching and performance.

Patterns in the lives of these five women composers parallel the lives of women composers in other ages. Their families respected music as a profession and pastime and therefore provided musical training. Each woman revealed promise in childhood and attracted artistic mentors. Each developed her talents through church music.

Other black American women composers have contributed to American music. These include Eva Jessye (b. 1895), choral director of the first production of George Gershwin's *Porgy and Bess*. She held the position through its run on Broadway and on its tour. Jessye has published several collections of spirituals. Her original compositions include a folk drama and her setting of *Paradise Lost and Regained* based on John Milton's well-known works.

Undine Smith Moore (b. 1906) is renowned for her choral compositions and arrangements of spirituals. For more than four decades she was a college professor of music theory and composition, and several of her students have achieved success as musicians. These include Billy Taylor of the Billy Taylor (Jazz) Trio and Leon Thompson, symphony conductor. Among Moore's original choral works are *Striving After God* and *Mother to Son*. Two notable choral arrangements of spirituals are *Fare Ye Well* and *Daniel, Daniel, Servant of the Lord*. She has also written instrumental chamber works.

Betty Jackson King (b. 1928), a recent president of the National Association of Negro Musicians, is a composer, choral conductor, pianist, and educator. Her compositions include a Biblical opera, Easter cantata, ballet, piano and organ works, instrumental works for violin and piano, cello, and voice and piano, and many choral compositions.

Jessye, Moore, and King further reveal the richness that awaits American music as black women composers develop their art in the paths of Price, Bonds, Perry, Pittman, and McLin.

Notes and References

Chapter One

1. Shirley Graham, "Spirituals to Symphonies," *Etude*, November, 1936, p. 691.
2. William P. Malm, *Music Cultures of the Pacific, the Near East, and Asia* (Englewood Cliffs, New Jersey: Prentice-Hall, 1967), p. 3. The sound of the bull-roarer indicates the presence of the supernatural to the peoples of the Arnhem land Aboriginal Reserve in Australia. Women may not approach.
3. Curt Sachs, *World History of the Dance* (New York: W. W. Norton, 1937), plate 1.
4. Sachs, *World History*, p. 212.
5. Sachs, *World History*, plate 1.
6. Curt Sachs, *The Rise of Music in the Ancient World, East and West* (New York: W. W. Norton, 1943), pp. 40–41.
7. Ralph Linton, *The Tree of Culture* (New York: Alfred A. Knopf, 1955), p. 333.
8. Sachs, *The Rise*, p. 81.
9. Lina Eckenstein, *Woman under Monasticism* (New York: Russell & Russell, 1963), pp. 216, 368, 378, and 382.
10. *Lieder von Hildegard von Bingen*, hrsg. von Pudentiana Barth, M. Immaculata Ritscher and Joseph Schmidt-Görg (Salzburg, 1969).
11. Peter Dronke, *The Medieval Lyric* (London: Hutchinson, 1968), p. 78.
12. Robert Eitner, *Biographisch-Bibliographisches Quellen-Lexicon der Musiker und Musikgelehrten* (Leipzig: Breitkopf and Haertel, 1898–1904).
13. Adriano Cavicchi, "Aleotti," *Die Musik in Geschichte und Gegenwart (MGG)*, Vol. 15, Suppl., (Kassel & Basel: Bärenreiter-Verlag, 1949–1973), cols. 130–131.
14. Phyllis Hartnoll, *The Concise History of Theatre* (New York: H. N. Abrams, 1968), p. 66.
15. Federico Ghisi, "Caccini," *MGG*, Vol. 2, cols. 609–612.
16. Claudio Sartori, "Strozzi," *MGG*, Vol. 12, cols. 1613–14.

17. Claudio Sartori, *Bibliografia della musica strumentale italiana stampata in Italia fino al 1700* (Firenze: L. S. Olschki, 1952).

18. Alfred Löwenberg, *Annals of Opera, 1597–1940*, "E. C. De La Guerre: Céphale et Procis." (2nd ed., Geneva: Societas Bibliographica, 1955), Vol. I, col. 95.

19. Felix Clément and Pierre Larousse, "Catherine ou La Belle Fermière" *Dictionnaire des Opéras*, (rev. ed., Paris, 1905), p. 206

20. Silvana Simonetti, "Agnesi," *MGG*, Vol. 15, col. 52.

21. Wilhelm Krabbe, "Anna Amalia" *MGG*, Vol. 1, col. 485.

22. Herbert Kupferberg, *The Mendelssohns, Three Generations of Genius* (New York: C. Scribner's Sons, 1972), p. 156.

23. He published three of her songs in his Op. 8 and three more in p. 9.

24. Georg Stieglitz, "Carreño," *MGG*, Vol. 2, col. 872.

25. Karl H. Wörner, "H. H. A. Beach," *MGG*, Vol. 1, col. 1457.

26. Burnet C. Tuthill, "Mrs. H. H. A. Beach," *Musical Quarterly*, Vol. 26 (1940), p. 297.

27. Jacques Chailley, "Boulanger," *MGG*, Vol. 15, p. 1005.

28. Linton, *The Tree of Culture*, pp. 425–426.

29. J. H. Nketia, *The Music of Africa* (New York: W. W. Norton, 1974), pp. 22–23.

30. Nketia, *The Music of Africa*, pp. 24–25.

31. Nketia, *The Music of Africa*, p. 34.

32. Sophie Drinker, *Music and Women* (New York: Coward-McCann, 1948), p. 31.

33. Drinker, *Music and Women*, p. 31.

34. Nketia, *The Music of Africa*, p. 38.

35. Nketia, *The Music of Africa*, p. 38.

36. Nketia, *The Music of Africa*, p. 61.

37. J. H. Nketia, "The Instrumental Resources of African Music," *Papers in African Studies*, Institute of African Studies, Legon (Accra, Ghana: Ghana Publishing Corp., n.d.), p. 16.

38. Nketia, "The Instrumental Resources," p. 2.

39. Nketia, "The Instrumental Resources," p. 18.

40. Eileen Southern, *The Music of Black Americans: A History* (New York: W. W. Norton, 1971), p. 55.

41. Southern, *The Music of Black Americans*, p. 109.

42. Zelma Watson George, "A Guide to Negro Music: An Annotated Bibliography of Negro Folk Music, and Art Music by Negro Composers or Based on Negro Thematic Material." (unpublished Doctoral dissertation, New York University, 1953), p. 104.

43. Harry A. Ploski, Otto J. Lindenmeyer, and Ernest Kaisen, eds.,

Reference Library of Black America, Vol. 4 (New York: Bellwether, 1971), p. 219.

44. Southern, *The Music of Black Americans*, pp. 254–55.

45. Southern, *The Music of Black Americans*, p. 305.

Chapter Two

1. In an interview with Neumon Leighton, close friend of Price, November 18, 1972.

2. Florence P. Robinson, daughter of Price, in a letter of June 20, 1973, to the author.

3. Robinson, in a letter of June 30, 1973.

4. Interview with Leighton.

5. Interview with Leighton.

6. Interview with Leighton.

7. Mrs. Lawrence Finn, former Little Rock music student of Price, in a letter of February 8, 1973, to the author.

8. Robinson, in a letter of June 20, 1973.

9. Robinson, in a letter of June 20, 1973.

10. Margaret Bonds, "A Reminiscence," *The Negro in Music and Art*, in *International Library of Negro Life and History* (New York: Publishers Co., 1968), Vol. 5, p. 192.

11. Interview with Leighton.

12. Shirley Graham, "Spirituals to Symphonies," *Etude*, November, 1936, p. 691.

13. Interview with Leighton.

14. Press comments on Price, supplied by Leighton.

15. Interview with Leighton, who explained that he was present when Price received the cable from England.

16. Press comments from Leighton.

17. Interview with Leighton.

18. Press comments from Leighton.

19. Price, in a letter of September, 1950, to Leighton.

20. Price, in a letter of September, 1950, to Leighton.

Chapter Three

1. Margaret Bonds, "A Reminiscence," *The Negro in Music and Art*, in *International Library of Negro Life and History* (New York: Publishers Co., 1968), Vol. 5, p. 192.

2. In an interview with Hortense Love, close friend of Margaret Bonds, who sang much of Bonds's music, May 18, 1973.

3. Bonds, "A Reminiscence," p. 191.

4. Bonds, "A Reminiscence," p. 192.

5. Will Marion Cook, in an undated letter to Bonds.

6. In an interview with Ruby Clark, May 18, 1973. She said Bonds had to walk down Marquette Road to visit her.

7. Interview with Clark.

8. In an interview with Nelmatilda Ritchie Woodard, close friend of Bonds and director, Division of Music, Chicago Public Schools, May 20, 1973.

9. In an interview with Theodore Charles Stone, past national president of NANM, concert singer, music critic, and close friend of Bonds, May 20, 1973.

10. Interview with Clark.

11. Interview with Clark.

12. In an interview with Bonds's husband and daughter, Lawrence and Djane Richardson, May 28, 1973.

13. Bonds, "A Reminiscence," p. 191.

14. Interview with Richardsons.

15. Interview with Love.

16. Hortense Love, notes for Margaret Bonds, *Five Spirituals*, (New York: Mutual Music Society, 1946.)

17. Interview with Richardsons.

18. Obituary for Margaret Bonds, *Jet*, May 18, 1972, p. 62.

19. The following citation appeared on the program: Truly a master musician, Margaret Bonds has given full measure of her special talent to the world. A "goodwill ambassador" extraordinary, she has been invited coast-to-coast in America and to foreign lands, including Russia and Africa, to hear her compositions performed by student choirs. She is a brilliant pianist, having an extensive background of concertizing with leading orchestras. Many of her works have been recorded by noted artists. The oustanding achievements of Margaret Bonds are a source of great pride to her alma mater.

20. Interview with Richardsons.

21. Bonds, "A Reminiscence," p. 192.

22. Bonds, "A Reminiscence," p. 192.

23. Interview with Clark.

24. Interview with Clark.

25. Bonds had written a treatise on Luther's life and hymns while she was a student at Northwestern University.

26. Program notes for "An All-Margaret Bonds Concert," Berean Baptist Church, Chicago, Illinois, January 31, 1967.
27. Interview with Richardsons.

Chapter Four

1. Julia Perry, in a letter of January 25, 1974, to the author.
2. Alumni records, Westminster Choir College, Princeton, New Jersey.
3. Perry, in a letter of January 25, 1974.
4. John Vinton, "Julia Perry," *Dictionary of Contemporary Music* (New York: E. P. Dutton & Co., 1974), p. 569.
5. Vinton, "Julia Perry," p. 569.
6. Anonymous record jacket notes for Julia Perry's *Homunculus C. F.* for 10 percussionists, Manhattan Percussion Ensemble, Paul Price conducting (Composers Recordings, Inc. CRI:SD-252).
7. Record jacket notes, *Homunculus C.F.*
8. Vincent F. Hopper, *Essentials of European Literature* (Great Neck, N.Y.: Barron's Educational Series), 1952, p. 412.
9. Hopper, *Essentials of European Literature*, p. 412.
10. Record jacket notes, *Homunculus C.F.*
11. Robert Sabin, review of Julia Perry's *Free At Last*, in *Musical America*, May, 1951, p. 26.
12. For a discussion of poetic forms common in black folk songs, see Eileen Southern, *The Music of Black Americans: A History* (New York: W. W. Norton & Co., 1971), pp. 189-192.
13. L. E. Cuyler, "Stabat Mater," *New Catholic Encyclopedia*, (edited by Most Rev. William J. McDonald, 1957), p. 626.
14. Cuyler, "Stabat Mater," p. 626.
15. Original Latin text in *Liber Usualis*, edited by the Benedictines of Solesmes, pp. 1634-37.

Chapter Five

1. In an interview with Pittman, August 1, 1972. She supplied biographical details for this chapter.
2. Interview with Pittman.
3. Written material supplied by Pittman, August 1, 1972.
4. Interview with Pittman.
5. "An Opera by Evelyn," *Daily Oklahoman*, May 30, 1954, Sunday Magazine, p. 17.

6. In an interview with Dean Harrison Kerr, July 20, 1972.

7. Aline Jean Treaner, "Warfield, Pittman and Choir Today," *Daily Oklahoman*, February 26, 1956.

8. Perdita Duncan, review of Evelyn Pittman's *Cousin Esther* in *New York Amsterdam News*, September 15, 1962.

9. Written material supplied by Pittman.

Chapter Six

1. In an interview with Lena McLin, March 24, 1973.

2. Interview with McLin.

3. Lena McLin, "Black Music in Church and School," in *Black Music in Our Culture*, edited by Dominique-Rene de Lerma (Kent, Ohio: Kent State University Press, 1970), p. 35.

4. McLin, "Black Music," p. 39.

5. Interview with McLin.

6. McLin, "Black Music," p. 40.

7. Interview with McLin.

8. Tom Glazer quotes this song in *Songs of Peace, Freedom and Protest* (New York: David McKay Co., 1970), pp. 332-333, as being an old union song first sung in 1931 by striking miners. "It is based on an old hymn, 'I Shall Not Be Moved,' itself based on a line from Jeremiah in the Bible, 'Blessed is the man who trusteth in the Lord, for he shall be as a tree planted by the waters.' " Bruce Jackson also cites the song in *Wake Up Dead Man: Afro-American Worksongs from Texas Prisons* (Cambridge, Massachusetts: Harvard University Press, 1972), p. 288. He comments that "Charlie Patton, in the early 20s, one of the most influential businessmen in the Mississippi Delta, recorded a very fine version of this song." A more modern version of it has been recorded: *We Shall Not Be Moved: Songs of the Freedom-Riders and the Sit-Ins* (Folkways GH-5591).

Bibliography

Primary Sources

1. Articles

BONDS, MARGARET. "A Reminiscence," *The Negro in Music and Art.*
in *International Library of Negro Life and History.* Edited by Lindsay
Patterson. New York: Publishers Co., 1968. (Vol. 5, pp. 191–193.)

McLIN, LENA. "Black Music in Church and School," in *Black Music in
our Culture.* Edited by Dominique-Rene de Lerma. Kent, Ohio: Kent
State University Press, 1970. (pp. 35–41.)

2. Interviews and Letters

McLIN, LENA. Personal interview. March 24–26, 1973; May 22, 1973.

PERRY, JULIA. Personal correspondence to author. (June 17, 1972; July
21, 1972; November 19, 1973; January 25, 1974.)

PITTMAN, EVELYN. Personal correspondence to author. (July, 1979;
February 12, 1980.)

———. Personal interview. August 1, 1972.

PRICE, FLORENCE. Personal correspondence to Neumon Leighton. (September, 1950.)

3. Musical Scores

BONDS, MARGARET. *The Ballad of the Brown King.* Words by Langston
Hughes. New York: Sam Fox Publishing Co., 1961.

———. *I Got a Home in That Rock.* New York: Beekman Music, 1968.

———. *The Negro Speaks of Rivers.* Words by Langston Hughes. New
York: Handy Brothers Music Co., 1946.

———. *Three Dream Portraits.* Words by Langston Hughes. New York:
G. Ricordi, 1959.

———. *To A Brown Girl Dead.* Words by Countee Cullen. Boston: R. D.
Row Music Co., 1956.

145

GLAZER, TOM. *Songs of Peace, Freedom and Protest.* New York: David McKay Co., 1970.

JACKSON, BRUCE. *Wake Up Dead Man: Afro-American Worksongs from Texas Prisons.* Cambridge, Massachusetts: Harvard University Press, 1972.

McLIN, LENA. *Free At Last.* Words by composer. Park Ridge, Illinois: General Words and Music Co., 1973.

————. *If They Ask You Why He Came.* Park Ridge, Illinois: General Words and Music Co., 1971.

————. *Let the People Sing Praise Unto the Lord.* Park Ridge, Illinois: General Words and Music Co., 1973.

————. *The Torch Has Been Passed.* Park Ridge, Illinois: General Words and Music Co., 1971.

PERGOLESI, GIOVANNI BATTISTA. *Stabat Mater.* New York: Edwin F. Kalmus.

PERRY, JULIA. *Free at Last.* New York: Galaxy Music Corp., 1951.

————. *Homunculus C. F.* New York: Southern Music Publishing Co., 1966.

————. *I'm a Poor Li'l Orphan in This Worl'.* New York: Galaxy Music Corp., 1952.

————. *Song of Our Saviour.* New York Galaxy Music Corp., 1953.

————. *Stabat Mater.* New York: Southern Music Publishing Co., 1954.

PITTMAN, EVELYN. *Anyhow.* New York: Carl Fischer, Inc., 1952.

————. *Nobody Knows de Trouble I See.* New York Carl Fischer, Inc., 1954.

————. *Rich Heritage.* Volume I. White Plains, New York: Evelyn Pittman, 1944; revised 1968.

————. *Rocka Mah Soul.* New York: Carl Fischer, Inc., 1952.

————. *Sit Down Servant.* New York: Carl Fischer, Inc. 1949.

PRICE, FLORENCE B. *An April Day.* New York: Handy Brothers Music Co., 1949.

————. *Moon Bridge.* Chicago: Gamble Hinged Music Co., 1930.

————. *My Soul's Been Anchored in the Lord.* New York: Carl Fischer, Inc., 1937.

————. *Songs to a Dark Virgin.* Words by Langston Hughes. New York: G. Schirmer, 1941.

————. *Three Little Negro Dances.* Bryn Mawr, Pennsylvania: Theodore Presser Co., 1933.

————. *Two Traditional Negro Spirituals.* New York: Handy Brothers Music Co., 1949.

ROSSINI, GIOACCHINO. *Stabat Mater.* New York: Edwin Kalmus.

Secondary Sources

1. Books

ABDUL, RAOUL. *Blacks in Classical Music.* New York: Dodd, Mead & Co., 1977.

An informal history of black musicians in the concert and opera world. Contains a chapter on black women in music including Florence B. Price, Margaret Bonds, and Julia Perry.

DE LERMA, DOMINIQUE-RENE. *Black Music in Our Culture.* Kent, Ohio: Kent State University Press, 1970.

Presents one article by Lena McLin. Other articles refer to Florence B. Price, Margaret Bonds, and Julia Perry.

DRINKER, SOPHIE. *Music and Women.* New York: Coward-McCann, 1948.

Traces the status of women in the history of the world. Also examines several reasons behind women's lack of prominence in the history of music. Discusses women in African societies and musical traditions.

DRONKE, PETER. *The Medieval Lyric.* London: Hutchinson, 1968.

Discusses the poetry of the Middle Ages. Hildegard of Bingen and other women poets are included.

ECKENSTEIN, LINA. *Woman under Monasticism.* New York: Russell and Russell, 1963.

A history of monasticism and religious orders for women. Contains chapters on saint-lore and convent life between A.D. 500 and A.D. 1500. First published in 1896.

EITNER, ROBERT. *Biographisch-Bibliographisches Quellen-Lexicon der Musiker und Musikgelehrten.* Leipzig: Breitkopf and Haertel, 1898–1904.

A bibliography of primary sources of music before 1800. Contains useful biographical information.

ELSON, ARTHUR. *Women's Work in Music.* Boston: L. C. Page & Co., 1903.

Describes woman's influence in music from ancient periods to the beginning of the twentieth century. Includes a summary of compositions by women composers from around the world; comparison of their works rank with those of male composers. No black women mentioned.

HARKNESS, GEORGIA. *Women in Church and Society*. Nashville: Abingdon Press, 1972.

Discusses Jewish and early Christian attitudes toward women.

HARTNOLL, PHYLLIS. *The Concise History of Theatre*. New York: H. N. Abrams, 1968.

Includes the role of women in the discussion of theatre history.

HIXON, DON L. and DON HENNESSEE. *Women in Music: A Bio-bibliography*. Metuchen, New Jersey: The Scarecrow Press, 1975.

A listing of biographies and bibliographic sources for more than 4,000 women in music from all countries and all periods of music, classified list of women musicians. Julia Perry is the only black woman composer cited. Other black women musicians such as Leontyne Price, Martina Arroya, and Natalie Hinderas listed.

HOPPER, VINCENT F. *Essentials of European Literature*. Great Neck, New York: Barron's Educational Series, 1952.

Discusses "The Homunculus" in Goethe's *Faust*. (Julia Perry based *Homunculus C. F.* on the experiment in *Faust* which created this being.)

KUPFERBERG, HERBERT. *The Mendelssohns, Three Generations of Genius*. New York: C. Scribner's Sons, 1972.

An account of the life and music of Fanny Mendelssohn is included in this biographical study of the family.

LAWRENCE, ANYA. *Women of Notes*. New York: Richards Rosen Press, 1978.

Includes 1,000 women composers born before 1900. Florence B. Price listed. Also has a chapter, "Survey of Women Composers Today," which mentions Julia Perry.

Liber Usualis. Tournai: Society of St. John the Evangelist, Declée, 1956.

Contains the Latin text of the *Stabat Mater*.

LINTON, RALPH. *The Tree of Culture*. New York: Alfred Knopf, 1955.

Traces the evolution of culture. Refers to women in Paleolithic cultures.

MALM, WILLIAM P. *Music Cultures of the Pacific, the Near East, and Asia.* Englewood Cliffs, New Jersey: Prentice-Hall, 1967.

Studies woman's role in the music of Egypt, Moslem Africa, and the Saharan Tuaregs.

NKETIA, J. H. *The Music of Africa.* New York: W. W. Norton & Co., 1974.

Discusses the musical roles of women in African society as well as African music and musical traditions.

PATTERSON, LINDSAY, ed. *The Negro in Music and Art,* in *International Library of Negro Life and History,* vol. 5. New York: Publishers Co., 1968.

One article in this anthology, "A Reminiscence," by Margaret Bonds, includes a review of several black musicians, composers, and poets who influenced her career. Florence B. Price is mentioned. Other articles examine black music and musicians.

ROACH, HILDRED. *Black American Music: Past and Present.* Boston: Crescendo Publishing Co., 1973.

Surveys black American musicians and music from colonial era to the present. Presents biographical sketches of Florence B. Price and Margaret Bonds. Julia Perry appears in a list of contemporary composers.

SACHS, CURT. *The Rise of Music in the Ancient World, East and West.* New York: W. W. Norton, 1943.

Discusses the music of primitive cultures. Refers to women in dance and music.

SACHS, CURT. *World History of the Dance.* New York: W. W. Norton, 1937.

Traces the development of dance in various cultures. The role of women in dance is included.

SKOWRONSKI, JOANN. *Women in American Music: A Bibliography.* Metuchen, New Jersey: The Scarecrow Press, 1978.

Annotated bibliography on American women in music from 1776 to

1976. Indicates sources for information about women in music. Black women composers Margaret Bonds and Undine Moore included.

SOUTHERN, EILEEN. *The Music of Black Americans: A History.* New York: W. W. Norton & Co., 1971.

Traces the history of black American music from the colonial period to today. Biographical sketches of Florence B. Price, Margaret Bonds, and Julia Perry presented.

STERN, SUSAN. *Women Composers: A Handbook.* Metuchen, New Jersey: The Scarecrow Press, 1978.

Catalogues women composers of classical music from the sixteenth century to the present from the United States and other countries. Includes Florence B. Price, Margaret Bonds, Julia Perry, Evelyn Pittman, and Lena McLin.

WILLIAMS, ORA. *American Black Women in the Arts and Social Sciences.* Metuchen, New Jersey: The Scarecrow Press, 1973.

Lists black women composers, their works, and publishers with bibliography of books and articles by and about black women in music.

2. Dictionaries and Encyclopedias

CLEMENT, FELIX and PIERRE LAROUSSE. *Dictionnaire des Opéras.* Paris, 1905.

Entries on French operas. In French, the articles are arranged alphabetically.

Die Musik in Geschichte und Gegenwart (MGG). Hrsg. von Friedrich Blume. Kassel and Basel: Bärenreiter-Verlag, 1949-1973.

A multivolume music reference work in German. Contains several articles on women in music. Includes biographical data and listing of compositions for composers, books for authors, and writings about individuals, places and topics.

LÖWENBERG, ALFRED. *Annals of Opera, 1597-1940,* Vol. I. Geneva: Societas Bibliographica, 1955.

A history of opera. Articles are arranged chronologically. Women composers and their works are included.

McDONALD, WILLIAM J., ed. *New Catholic Encyclopedia.* New York: McGraw-Hill Book Co., 1957.

Contains an article on the *Stabat Mater* by L. E. Cuyler.

VINTON, JOHN, ed. *Dictionary of Contemporary Music.* New York: E. P. Dutton & Co., 1974.

Includes a biographical sketch of Julia Perry with a brief listing of her compositions.

3. Articles in Periodicals and Collections

Obituary for Julia Perry, *The Black Perspective in Music,* (Fall 1979), p. 282.

CASWELL, AUSTIN. "What is Black Music?," *Music Journal,* October, 1969, p. 31.

Discusses contributions by black musicians and the need for the inclusion of black music and musicians in schools by music educators.

GRAHAM, SHIRLEY. "Spirituals to Symphonies," *Etude,* November, 1936, p. 691.

Reviews the progress of black musicians since slavery. Presents a biographical sketch of Florence B. Price.

Obituary for Margaret Bonds, *Jet,* XLIII (May 18, 1972), p. 62.

NKETIA, J. H. "The Instrumental Resources of African Music," in *Papers in African Studies* No. 3. Edited by Institute of African Studies, Legon. Accra, Ghana: Ghana Publishing Corp. (p. 16.)

Examines the origin, usage, development, and distribution of African musical instruments. Refers to the role of women in the use of various instruments and techniques of performance.

TUTHILL, BURNET C. "Mrs. H. H. A. Beach," *Musical Quarterly,* Vol. 26, 1940.

Discusses the life and musical contributions of Mrs. Beach.

YUHASZ, Sister MARIE JOY, O. P. "Black Composers and Their Piano Music," *The American Music Teacher,* 19 (February/March, 1970).

Studies the piano works of five black composers, including Florence B. Price and Margaret Bonds. Brief biography, lists of works, and an analytical discussion of the piano works presented on each composer.

4. Unpublished Sources

GEORGE, ZELMA WATSON. "A Guide to Negro Music: An Annotated Bibliography of Negro Folk Music and Art Music by Negro Composers or Based on Negro Thematic Material." Unpublished doctoral dissertation. New York University, 1953.

A critical review of the literature about black music and the problems of research. One section presents information about black musicians of the slavery period. Several women included.

McCANN, SHIRLEY GRAHAM. "The Survival of Africanism in Modern Music." Unpublished master's thesis. Oberlin College, 1934.

Includes biographical data on Florence B. Price and a brief analysis by Price of her first symphony.

5. Interviews and Letters

CLARK, RUBY. Personal interview about Margaret Bonds. May 18, 1973; May 20, 1973.

COOK, WILL MARION. Personal correspondence to Margaret Bonds. (1941.)

FINN, Mrs. LAWRENCE. Personal correspondence to present writer about Florence B. Price. (February 8, 1973.)

KERR, HARRISON. Personal interview about Evelyn Pittman. July 20, 1972.

LEIGHTON, NEUMON. Personal interview about Florence B. Price. November 18, 1973.

LOVE, HORTENSE. Personal interview about Margaret Bonds. May 18, 1973.

RICHARDSON, DJANE and LAWRENCE RICHARDSON. Personal interview about Margaret Bonds. May 28, 1973.

ROBINSON, FLORENCE P[RICE]. Personal correspondence to present writer about Florence B. Price. (June 20, 1973.)

STONE, THEODORE CHARLES. Personal interview about Margaret Bonds. May 20, 1973.

WOODARD, NELMATILDA RITCHIE. Personal interview about Margaret Bonds. May 20, 1973.

6. Miscellaneous Sources

Alumni Records, Westminster Choir College, Princeton, New Jersey.

Information about Julia Perry as a student and her career as composer and conductor.

ANON. Record jacket notes for Julia Perry's *Homunculus C. F.* for 10 percussionists, Manhattan Percussion Ensemble, Paul Price, conductor. Composer Recordings, Inc., CRI-SD252.

Includes biography and the composer's description of the composition.

FLANAGAN, WILLIAM. Album notes for Julia Perry's *Stabat Mater*, Makiko Asakura, mezzo-soprano, Japan Philharmonic Symphony Orchestra, William Strickland, conductor. Composer Recordings, Inc., CRI–133.

Contains biographical sketch with description of the composition.

LOVE, HORTENSE. Notes for *Five Spirituals*, arranged by Margaret Bonds. New York: Mutual Music Society, 1946.

Gives background on the spiritual melodies in the collection.

"An Opera by Evelyn." *Daily Oklahoman* (Oklahoma City). May 30, 1954, Magazine section.

Biographical information on Evelyn Pittman with discussion of her opera *Cousin Esther.*

Program Notes. "An All-Margaret Bonds Concert." Presented at the Berean Baptist Church, Chicago, Illinois. January 31, 1967.

Includes a biographical sketch of Bonds with a listing of works.

TREANOR, ALINE JEAN. "Warfield, Pittman and Choir Today." *Daily Oklahoman* (Oklahoma City), February 26, 1956.

Contains biographical data on Evelyn Pittman.

Catalogue of Musical Works

This catalogue lists works obtained from the publicity files of the composers, publishers' catalogues, the American Society of Composers, Authors, and Publishers (ASCAP), the Library of Congress, programs, program notes, and reviews of works. I have attempted to present a comprehensive catalogue; however, limited general access to the family collections, especially the Price collection, has precluded this. We need further investigation of private collections holding unpublished manuscripts to confirm the completeness of these listings.

To the left of the works is the publication date or the completion date in chronological order.

1. Published Works

1928 PRICE, FLORENCE B. *Anticipation,* for piano. Chicago: McKinley Publishers,

———. *Doll Waltz,* for piano. Chicago: McKinley Publishers.

———. *The Waltzing Fairy,* for piano. Chicago: McKinley Publishers.

———. *Zephry* (Mexican folk song), for piano. Chicago: McKinley Publishers.

1930 PRICE, FLORENCE B. *Moon Bridge* (words by Mary Rolofson Gamble), for voice and piano. Chicago: Gamble Hinged Music Co.

1933 PRICE, FLORENCE B. *Three Little Negro Dances:* "Hoe Cake," "Rabbit Foot," "Ticklin' Toes," for piano. Bryn Mawr, Pennsylvania: Theodore Presser Co.

1935 PRICE, FLORENCE B. *A Sachem's Pipe,* for piano. New York: Carl Fischer.

———. *Tecumseh,* for piano. New York: Carl Fischer.

1936 PRICE, FLORENCE B. *The Butterfly,* for piano. New York: Carl Fischer.

———. *The Gnat and the Bee,* for piano. New York: Carl Fischer.

———. *The Rose,* for piano. New York: Carl Fischer.

1937 PRICE, FLORENCE B. *Bright Eyes* for piano. Bryn Mawr, Pennsylvania: Theodore Presser Co.

————. *Cabin Song*, for piano. Bryn Mawr, Pennsylvania: Theodore Presser Co.

————. *Levee Dance*, for piano. Bryn Mawr, Pennsylvania: Theodore Presser Co.

————. *Morning Sunbeam*, for piano. Bryn Mawr, Pennsylvania: Theodore Presser Co.

————. *Nobody Knows the Trouble I See*, for piano. Bryn Mawr, Pennsylvania: Theodore Presser Co.

————. *My Soul's Been Anchored in de Lord*, for voice and piano; voice and orchestra. New York: Carl Fischer.

1939 BONDS, MARGARET. *Georgia* (with Andy Razof and Joe Davis), for voice and piano (popular song). New York: Dorsey Bros. Music Corp.

————. *Peachtree Street*, for voice and piano (popular song). New York: Dorsey Bros. Music Corp.

PRICE, FLORENCE B. *Three Little Negro Dances*, for band. Bryn Mawr, Pennsylvania: Theodore Presser Co.

1940 BONDS, MARGARET. *Three Sheep in a Pasture*, for voice and piano. New York: Clarence Williams Music Co.

1941 BONDS, MARGARET. *Spring Will Be So Sad* (with H. Dickinson), (popular song). New York: Mutual Music Society.

PRICE, FLORENCE B. *Songs to a Dark Virgin* (words by Langston Hughes), for voice and piano. New York: G. Schirmer.

1942 BONDS, MARGARET. *Children's Sleep* (words by Vernon Glasser), for SATB chorus and piano. New York: Carl Fischer.

PRICE, FLORENCE B. *Cotton Dance*, for piano. New York: Carl Fischer, Inc.; *Oxford Piano Course*, Fifth Book, Oxford University Press.

————. *Were You There When They Crucified My Lord*, for piano. New York: Carl Fischer, Inc.; *Oxford Piano Course*, Fifth Book, Oxford University Press.

1944 PITTMAN, EVELYN. *Rich Heritage*, Volume I (songs and stories about outstanding black Americans) for elementary level. White Plains, New York: Evelyn Pittman, (revised-1968).

1946 BONDS, MARGARET. *Five Spirituals* ("Dry Bones," "Sit Down Servant," "Lord I Just Can't Keep From Crying," "You Can Tell the World," also for voice and orchestra; "I'll Reach to Heaven"), for voice and piano. New York: Mutual Music Society.

————. *The Negro Speaks of Rivers* (words by Langston Hughes), for voice and piano. New York: Handy Brothers Music Co.

PRICE, FLORENCE B. *Night* (words by Louise C. Wallace), for voice and piano. New York: Edward B. Marks Music Corp.

————. *Out of the South Blew a Wind* (words by Fanny Carter Woods), for voice and piano. New York: Edward B. Marks Music Corp.

1947　PERRY, JULIA. *Carillon Heigh-Ho* (words by composer), for mixed chorus and piano. New York: Carl Fischer.

PRICE, FLORENCE B. *Clover Blossom*, for piano. Chicago: McKinley Publishers.

————. *Here and There*, for piano. Chicago: McKinley Publishers.

————. *Criss Cross*, for piano. Chicago: McKinley Publishers.

————. *March of the Beetles*, for piano. Chicago: McKinley Publishers.

————. *Rock-a-bye*, for piano. Chicago: McKinley Publishers.

————. *Witch of the Meadow* for SSA chorus. Chicago: Gamble Hinged Music Co.

1949　PERRY, JULIA. *Lord, What Shall I Do?*, for voice and piano. Boston: McLaughlin and Reilly Co.

PITTMAN, EVELYN. *Sit Down Servant*, for SATB chorus, alto, and baritone solos a cappella. New York: Carl Fischer.

PRICE, FLORENCE B. *An April Day* (words by Joseph F. Cotter), for voice and piano. New York: Handy Brothers Music Co.

————. *Heav'n Bound Soldier*, for SSA chorus and piano. New York: Handy Brothers Music Co.

————. *Three Little Negro Dances*, for two pianos. Bryn Mawr, Pennsylvania: Theodore Presser Co.

————. *Two Traditional Negro Spirituals* ("I'm Bound for the Kingdom," "I'm Workin' on my Buildin'."), for voice and piano. New York: Handy Brothers Music Co.

1950　PERRY, JULIA. *By the Sea* (words by composer), for voice and piano. New York: Galaxy Music Corp.

PRICE, FLORENCE B. *Moon Bridge*, for women's chorus. New York: Remick Music Co.

1951　PERRY, JULIA. *Free At Last*, for voice and piano. New York: Galaxy Music Corp.

————. *Our Thanks to Thee* (words by composer), for mixed chorus, contralto solo, and organ. New York: Galaxy Music Corp.

PITTMAN, EVELYN. *We Love America*, for SATB chorus. Oklahoma City: Evelyn Pittman.

PRICE, FLORENCE B. *The Goblin and the Mosquito,* for solo piano; piano duet. Chicago: Clayton F. Summy Music Co.

———. *In Quiet Mood,* for organ. New York: Galaxy Music Corp.

———. *The Old Boatman,* for piano. Chicago: Clayton F. Summy Co.

———. *The Sea Swallow,* for piano. Chicago: Clayton F. Summy Co.

1952 PERRY, JULIA. *I'm a Poor Li'l Orphan in the Worl',* for voice and piano. New York: Galaxy Music Corp.

———. *Short Piece,* for orchestra. New York: Peer-Southern Organization.

———. *Ye Who Seek the Lord,* for mixed chorus and tenor solo. New York: Galaxy Music Corp.

PITTMAN, EVELYN. *Anyhow,* for SATB chorus a cappella. New York: Carl Fischer.

———. *Rocka Mah Soul,* for SATB chorus and baritone solo a cappella. New York: Carl Fisher.

1953 PERRY JULIA. *Be Merciful Unto Me,* for mixed chorus. New York: Galaxy Music Corp.

———. *How Beautiful Are the Feet,* for voice and piano. New York: Galaxy Music Corp.

———. *Song of Our Saviour,* for mixed chorus. New York: Galaxy Music Corp.

PRICE, FLORENCE B. *Dances in the Canebrakes,* for piano. Los Angeles: Affiliated Musicians.

———. *Nature's Magic,* for SSA chorus and piano. Chicago: Clayton F. Summy Co.

1954 PERRY, JULIA. *Stabat Mater,* for contralto and string orchestra or string quartet. New York: Southern Music Co.

PITTMAN, EVELYN. *Nobody Knows de Trouble I See,* for SATB chorus and unspecified solo a cappella. New York: Carl Fischer.

1955 PITTMAN, EVELYN. *Joshua,* for SATB chorus, soli, and piano. New York: Carl Fischer.

1956 BONDS, MARGARET. *Rainbow Gold* (words by Roger Chaney), for voice and piano. New York: Chappelle and Co.

———. *To a Brown Girl Dead* (words by Countee Cullen), for voice and piano. Boston: R. D. Row Music Co.

1957 BONDS, MARGARET. *You Can Tell the World,* for SATB chorus and piano (also SSA, TTBB, SATB unaccompanied, arr. by Charles N. Smith). New York: Mutual Music Society.

PRICE, FLORENCE B. *Song for Snow,* for SATB chorus and piano.

New York: Carl Fischer.

1959 BONDS, MARGARET. *Ezek'el Saw the Wheel,* for voice and piano; voice and orchestra. New York: Beekman Music.

———. *I Got a Home in that Rock,* for voice and piano; voice and orchestra. New York: Beekman Music. (Re-issued 1968).

———. *Three Dream Portraits:* "Minstrel Man," "Dream Variation," "I, Too," (words by Langston Hughes), for voice and piano. New York: G. Ricordi.

1960 BONDS, MARGARET. *Sing Aho,* for voice and piano. New York: Chappelle and Co.

1961 BONDS, MARGARET. *The Ballad of the Brown King* (Christmas cantata - libretto by Langston Hughes), for SATB chorus, soli, and piano. New York: Sam Fox Publishing Co.

PITTMAN, EVELYN. *Trampin',* for SATB chorus a cappella. Stamford, Connecticut: Jack Spratt Music Co.

1962 BONDS, MARGARET. *Go Tell It On the Mountain,* for voice and piano, SATB chorus a cappella. New York: Beekman Music.

———. *Hold On,* for voice and piano; voice and orchestra. New York: Beekman Music.

———. *Mary Had a Little Baby* (from *The Ballad of the Brown King*), for piano. New York: Sam Fox Publishing Co.

———. *The Negro Speaks of Rivers,* for SATB chorus and piano. New York: Handy Brothers Music Co.

PERRY, JULIA. *Pastoral,* for flute and string quartet. New York: Southern Music Co.

1963 BONDS, MARGARET. *He's Got the Whole World in His Hands,* for voice and piano; voice and orchestra. New York: Beekman Music.

———. *Mary Had a Little Baby* (from *The Ballad of the Brown King*), for women's chorus. New York: Sam Fox Publishing Co.

1965 PERRY, JULIA. *Second Piano Concerto,* for piano and orchestra. New York: Peer-Southern Organization.

1966 BONDS, MARGARET. *Ezek'el Saw the Wheel,* for SATB chorus and piano. New York: Mercury Music Corp.

———. *I Shall Pass Through the World,* for voice and piano. New York: Bourne Co.

PERRY, JULIA. *Homunculus C. F.,* for ten percussionists, harp, and piano. New York: Southern Music Publishing Co.

———. *Symphony No. 6,* for band. New York: Carl Fischer.

———. *Violin Concerto,* for violin and orchestra. New York: Carl

Fischer.

McLIN, LENA. *Glory, Glory Hallelujah,* for SATB chorus, soprano solo, and piano. Park Ridge, Illinois: Neil A. Kjos Music Co.

1967 BONDS, MARGARET. *Didn't It Rain,* for voice and piano. New York: Beekman Music Co.

———. *Joshua Fit da Battle of Jericho,* for voice and piano; voice and orchestra. New York: Beekman Music.

———. *Troubled Water,* for piano. New York: Sam Fox Publishing Co.

McLIN, LENA. *All the Earth Sing Unto the Lord,* for SATB chorus a cappella. Park Ridge, Illinois: Neil A. Kjos Music Co.

———. *Cert'nly Lord, Cert'nly Lord,* for SATB chorus, soprano or tenor solo a cappella. Park Ridge, Illinois: Neil A. Kjos Music Co.

———. *Writ'en Down My Name,* for SATB chorus and baritone solo a cappella. Park Ridge, Illinois: Neil A. Kjos Music Co.

1968 PITTMAN, EVELYN. *Rich Heritage,* Volume I (songs and stories about outstanding black Americans), for elementary level. White Plains, New York: Evelyn Pittman, (First published, Oklahoma City, 1944).

1969 McLIN, LENA. *The Earth is the Lord's,* for SATB chorus. Westbury, New York: Pro Art Publications.

———. *Is There Anybody Here,* for SATB chorus and piano. Westbury, New York: Pro Art Publications.

———. *I Want Jesus to Walk With Me,* for SATB chorus and piano. Westbury, New York: Pro Art Publications.

———. *Lit'le Lamb, Lit'le Lamb,* for SATB chorus and soprano solo a cappella. Park Ridge, Illinois: Neil A. Kjos Music Co.

1970 BONDS, MARGARET. *Bright Star,* for voice and piano. California: Pasea.

McLIN, LENA. *In This World* (collection with words by composer, except *I Love No One But You, Baby* by Beverly McLin and Nathaniel McLin). Park Ridge, Illinois: General Words and Music Co.

1971 McLIN, LENA. *The Colors of the Rainbow* (words by composer), for SATB chorus and piano. Westbury, New York: Pro Art Publications, Inc.

———. *Done Made My Vow to the Lord,* for SATB chorus and baritone solo. Park Ridge, Illinois: Neil A. Kjos Music Co.

———. *For Jesus Christ is Born,* for SATB chorus a cappella. Park Ridge, Illinois: Neil A. Kjos Music Co.

————. *I Am Somebody*, for SATB chorus, narrator, and piano. New York: Edward B. Marks Music Corp.

————. *If They Ask You Why He Came* (words by composer), for SATB chorus and piano. Park Ridge, Illinois: General Words and Music Co.

————. *If We Could Exchange Places* (words by composer), for SATB chorus, flute, electric piano, and electric bass guitar. New York: Marks Music Corp.

————. *I'm Moving Up* (words by composer), for SATB chorus and piano. New York: Sildet Music Co.

————. *The Little Baby* (words by composer), for SATB chorus, optional solo, and piano. Park Ridge, Illinois: Neil A. Kjos Music Co.

————. *Psalm 100*, for SATB chorus a cappella. Westbury, New York: Pro Art Publications.

————. *Psalm 117*, for SATB chorus and piano or organ. Westbury, New York: Pro Art Publications.

————. *Sanctus and Benedictus*, for SATB chorus and piano. Park Ridge, Illinois: General Words and Music Co.

————. *The Torch Has Been Passed* (words by composer—based on a text by President John F. Kennedy), for SATB chorus a cappella. Park Ridge, Illinois: General Words and Music Co.

————. *We've Just Got to Have Peace All Over This World* (words by composer), for SATB chorus and piano. New York: Sildet Music Co.

————. *What Will You Put Under Your Christmas Tree?* (words by composer), for SATB chorus and piano. Park Ridge, Illinois: General Words and Music Co.

1972 McLIN, LENA. *Eucharist of the Soul*, Liturgical Mass, for SATB chorus and piano or organ. Park Ridge, Illinois: General Words and Music Co.

————. *Friendship* (song cycle):"Friendship" (words by Ali Ben Abu Taheb); "Fair Weather Friend" (words by William Shakespeare); "I'll Be Your Friend" (words by composer), for SATB chorus and piano. Park Ridge, Illinois: General Words and Music Co.

————. *Gwendolyn Brooks: A Musical Portrait* (words by composer), for SATB chorus and piano. Park Ridge, Illinois: General Words and Music Co.

————. *My God is So High*, for SATB chorus a cappella. Park Ridge, Illinois: Neil A. Kjos Music Co.

————. *New Born King* (words by composer), for SATB chorus a cappella. Park Ridge, Illinois: General Words and Music Co.

1973 McLIN, LENA. *Free At Last*—"A Portrait of Martin Luther King, Jr." (words by composer), for SATB chorus, soprano and baritone or mezzo soprano solo, narrator, and piano. Park Ridge, Illinois: General Words and Music Co.

————. *Let the People Sing Praise Unto the Lord*, for SATB chorus, piano or organ, and B♭ trumpet. Park Ridge, Illinois: General Words and Music Co.

1974 McLIN, LENA. *I'm So Glad Trouble Don't Last Always*, for SATB chorus and piano. Park Ridge, Illinois: Neil A. Kjos Music Co.

————. *Winter, Spring, Summer, Autumn* (words by composer), song cycle for SATB chorus and piano. Park Ridge, Illinois: Neil A. Kjos Music Co.

1976 McLIN, LENA. *Challenge*, for SATB chorus, piano, optional trumpet, tenor sax, bass guitar, drums. Park Ridge, Illinois: General Words and Music Co.

1978 McLIN, LENA. *Give Me that Old Time Religion*, for SATB chorus a cappella. Park Ridge, Illinois: General Words and Music Co.

————. *Now that We're Leaving*, for SATB chorus and piano. Park Ridge, Illinois: General Words and Music Co.

————. *Two Introits*, for SATB chorus and piano. Park Ridge, Illinois: General Words and Music Co.

————. *You and I Together*, for SATB chorus and piano. Park Ridge, Illinois: General Words and Music Co.

2. Published Works (undated)

PRICE, FLORENCE B. *Adoration*, for organ. Dayton, Ohio: Lorenz Publishing Co.————. *Annie Laurie*, for piano duet. Chicago: McKinley Publishers.

————. *At the Cotton Gin*, for piano. New York: G. Schirmer.

————. *By Candlelight*, for violin and piano. Chicago: McKinley Publishers.

————. *The Deserted Garden*, for violin and piano. Bryn Mawr, Pennsylvania: Theodore Presser Co.

————. *The Engine*, for piano. Chicago: McKinley Publishers.

————. *Evening Song*, for organ. New York: Galaxy Music Corp.

————. *Mellow Twilight*, for violin and piano. Chicago: McKinley Publishers.

————. *New Moon*, for women's chorus with optional soprano obbligato and four-hand accompaniment. Chicago: Gamble Hinged Music Co.

———. *Offertory*, for organ. Dayton, Ohio: Lorenz Publishing Co.

———. *Playful Rondo*, for violin and piano. Chicago: McKinley Publishers.

———. *Silent Night*, for piano duet. Chicago: McKinley Publishers.

———. *The Waterfall*, for piano. Chicago: McKinley Publishers.

BONDS, MARGARET. *Empty Interlude* (popular song), for voice and piano. New York: Robbins Music Co.

———. *Mary Had a Little Baby* from *The Ballad of the Brown King* (words by Langston Hughes), for voice and piano. New York: Sam Fox Publishing Co.

PERRY, JULIA. *The Cask of Amontillado*, one act opera adapted from the story by Edgar Allan Poe with libretto in English, German, and Italian by the composer; in collaboration with Virginia Card. New York: Peer-Southern Organization.———. *Frammenti Dalle Lettere de "Santa Caterina,"* fragments from the Letter of St. Catherine, Italian text, for mixed chorus, soprano solo, and small orchestra. New York: Southern Music Co.

———. *Hommage to Vivaldi*, for orchestra. New York: Peer-Southern Organization.

PITTMAN, EVELYN. *I Love the Springtime*, for SATB chorus and piano. Oklahoma City: Evelyn Pittman.

3. Unpublished Works (dated)

1931 BONDS, MARGARET. *A Dance in Brown*, for piano (received Honorable Mention in Rodman Wanamaker Music Composition Contest).

1932 BONDS, MARGARET. *Sea Ghost*, for voice and piano (received First Prize in Rodman Wanamaker Music Composition Contest).

———. *Sleep Song* (words by Joyce Kilmer), for voice and piano.

PRICE, FLORENCE B. *Ethiopia's Shadow in America*, for orchestra (received Honorable Mention in Rodman Wanamaker Music Composition Contest).

———. *Fantasie No. 4*, for piano (received Honorable Mention in Rodman Wanamaker Music Composition Contest).

———. *Sonata in E Minor* for piano (received First Prize in Rodman Wanamaker Music Composition Contest).

1934 PRICE, FLORENCE B. *Concerto in d Minor*, for piano and orchestra.

————. *Concerto in f Minor,* for piano and orchestra.

1936 BONDS, MARGARET. *Joy* (words by Langston Hughes), for voice and piano.

1940 PRICE, FLORENCE B. *Symphony No. 3 in c Minor,* for orchestra.

1947 PERRY, JULIA. *Deep Sworn Vow,* for voice and piano.

————. *Is There Anybody Here,* for women's voices.

————. *King Jesus Lives,* for voice and piano.

————. *Lament,* for piano.

————. *Pearls on Silk,* for piano.

————. *Suite of Shoes,* for piano.

————. *The Lord is Risen,* for men's voices.

————. *To Electra,* for voice and piano.

1948 PERRY, JULIA. *Chicago* (secular cantata after Carl Sandburg's poems), for mixed chorus, baritone solo, narrator, and orchestra.

1950 PERRY, JULIA. *Ruth,* sacred cantata for mixed chorus and organ.

1952 PERRY, JULIA. *Study for Orchestra* (premiered in Italy by the Turin Symphony Orchestra, conducted by Dean Dixon; performed by New York Philharmonic Orchestra in 1965).

1954 PITTMAN, EVELYN. *Cousin Esther,* opera (revised in 1956).

1956 BONDS, MARGARET. *African Dance,* duet (words by Langston Hughes.)

1957 McLIN, LENA. *Impressions for Piano.*

1959 BONDS, MARGARET. *Shakespeare in Harlem,* stage work-music (Langston Hughes-Robert Glenn Production).

PERRY, JULIA. *Requiem for Orchestra.*

————. *Symphony No. 1,* for orchestra.

1960 BONDS, MARGARET. *Migration,* ballet.

————. *Songs of the Seasons* (from Fields of Wonder by Langston Hughes, song cycle for male chorus. "Heaven," "Snail," "Big Sun," "Moonlight Night," "Carmel," "Snake," "New Moon," "Birth."

1962 PERRY, JULIA. *Symphony No. 3,* for orchestra.

1963 BONDS, MARGARET. *Stopping By the Woods on a Snowy Evening,* for voice and piano.

————. *When the Dove Enters In* (words by Langston Hughes), for voice and piano.

PERRY, JULIA. *Contretemps,* for orchestra.

————. *Violin Concerto,* for violin and orchestra.

McLIN, LENA. *And She Took A Ring and Placed it on His Finger* (inspired by Jacqueline Kennedy), for voice and piano.

1964 BONDS, MARGARET. *Troubled Water*, for cello and piano.
      PERRY, JULIA. *The Selfish Giant*, three-act opera-ballet.
      ———. *Symphony No. 4*, for orchestra.
1965 PERRY, JULIA. *Piano Concerto*, for piano and orchestra.
      ———. *Symphony No. 9*, for orchestra.
1966 BONDS, MARGARET. *What Lips My Lips Have Kissed* (words by
      Edna St. Vincent Millay), for voice and piano.
1967 PERRY, JULIA. *Symphony U.S.A.*, for chorus and small orchestra.
1968 BONDS, MARGARET. *Don't Speak* (words by Janice Lovoos), for
      voice and piano.
      ———. *Pot Pouri* (words by Janice Lovoos), six songs for voice and
      piano: "Will There Be Enough," "Go Back to Leanna," "Touch
      the Hem of His Garment," "Bright Star," "No Man Has Seen
      His Face," "Animal Rock 'n Roll."
      PERRY, JULIA. *Symphony No. 8*, for orchestra.
1970 BONDS, MARGARET. *Burlesque is Alive*, music for stage work
      (Inner City Repertory Co. production, Los Angeles).
      ———. *Ev'ry Time I Feel the Spirit*, for voice and piano.
      ———. *Hold the Wind*, for voice and piano.
      ———. *I Wish I Knew How It Would Feel to Be Free*, for mixed chorus
      and soprano solo.
      ———. *No Man Has Seen His Face*, for SATB chorus.
      ———. *Run Sinner Run*, for voice and piano.
      ———. *Sinner Please Don't Let This Harvest Pass*, for voice and piano;
      SATB chorus and soprano solo.
      ———: *Standing in the Need of Prayer*, for SATB chorus and soprano
      solo.
      ———. *This Little Light of Mine*, for voice and piano.
1971 PITTMAN, EVELYN. *Freedom Child*, music drama.
1972 BONDS, MARGARET. *Credo*, for chorus and orchestra, (premiered
      April 1972 by Los Angeles Symphony Orchestra, conducted by
      Zubin Mehta).
1977 PITTMAN, EVELYN. *Jim Noble*, music drama.

4. Unpublished Works (undated)

BONDS, MARGARET. *Mass in d Minor* (Latin text), for chorus and
      orchestra.———. *The Nile Fantasy*, for piano and orchestra.
      ———. *The Pasture* (words by Robert Frost), for voice and piano.
      ———. *Peter and the Bells*, symphony, for orchestra.
      ———. *Romey and Julie*, musical comedy.
      ———. *Spiritual Suite for Piano:* "The Valley of Bones," (based on "Dry

Bones"); "The Bells," (based on "Peter Go Ring Dem Bells"); "Group Dance," (based on "Wade in the Water").

———. *Tropics After Dark* (American Negro Exposition), music for stage work.

———. *Troubled Island* (words by Langston Hughes), music for stage work.

———. *U.S.A.*, incidental music (based on works by John Dos Passos).

———. *Wings Over Broadway*, ballet.

———. *Winter Night's Dream*, music for stage work.

McLIN, LENA. *The Advent*, Christmas cantata, for SATB chorus and soprano, alto, and tenor solos.

———. *The Agreement*, marriage cantata.

———. *The Ascension*, Easter cantata, for SATB chorus, soprano, and tenor solos.

———. *Bancroft*, opera for mezzo soprano, two baritones, tenor, contralto, and SATB chorus.

———. *Burden Down*, for SATB chorus.

———. *The Church Cantata*, for SATB chorus, narrator, piano, and chimes.

———. *Comment*, rock opera.

———. *Done Made My Vow to the Lord*, for voice and piano.

———. *Don't Let Nobody Turn You Around*, for voice and piano.

———. *Down By the River*, for voice and piano.

———. *Gay* (words by Paul Lawrence Dunbar), for baritone voice and piano.

———. *Give Me Jesus*, for SATB chorus.

———. *Give Me That Old Time Religion*, for voice and piano.

———. *God Made Us All*, for SATB chorus.

———. *Gonna Rise Up in the Kingdom*, for voice and piano.

———. *Humpty Dumpty*, opera.

———. *I Cannot Believe* (words by composer), for voice and piano.

———. *If I Could Give You All I Have*, for voice and piano.

———. *I Heard the Preaching of the Elders*, for SATB chorus.

———. *I'm Gonna Make it Anyway* (popular song), for voice and piano.

———. *Impressions No. 1*, for orchestra.

———. *I'm So Glad Trouble Don't Last Always*, for voice and piano.

———. *I Wish That I Could Hear You Say* (popular song), for voice and piano.

———. *Jesus Stayed in the Wilderness*, for SATB chorus.

———. *The Johnny Coleman Cantata*, for SATB chorus, baritone solo, and narrator.

————. *Judas*, for SATB chorus.

————. *Keep Silence*, for SATB chorus.

————. *Lord, Oh Hear Me Praying*, for voice and piano.

————. *Low Down the Chariot Let Me Ride*, for voice and piano.

————. *Missa Nigra*, folk mass.

————. *Now That I've Come to You* (popular song).

————. *O Sing*, for SATB chorus.

————. *Out of the Depths Have I Cried Unto You*, for SATB chorus.

————. *Psalm 113*, for SATB chorus.

————. *Psalm 124*, for SATB chorus.

————. *St. Raymond the Pinafold*, liturgical mass.

————. *Silence* (words by Paul Lawrence Dunbar), for voice and piano.

————. *Song Cycle* (words by composer): "On Money Passing Through Our Hands," "On Why Didn't We," "On Didn't We," "On It's Not Too Late," for voice and piano.

————. *Song in c Minor*, for piano.

————. *Steady, Jesus Listening*, for SATB chorus.

————. *The Stoning of Stephen*, cantata for SATB chorus, baritone solo, and narrator.

————. *A Summer Day*, for piano.

————. *When Jesus Met the Woman at the Well*, for SATB chorus.

————. *Who Knowest Whether Thou Art Comest to the Kingdom*, for SATB chorus.

————. *Why Don't You Give Up the World?*

————. *The Year's At the Spring*, for voice and piano.

————. *You Better Rise Women, Face the Challenge* (written for a Women's Day program), for women's voices.

PERRY, JULIA. *The Bottle*, opera.

————. *Episode*, for orchestra.

————. *Missa Brevis*, for mixed chorus and organ.

————. *Seven Contrasts*, for baritone and chamber ensemble.

————. *Symphony No. 12*, "Simple symphony," for orchestra.

————. *Three Piano Pieces for Children.*

————. *Three Warnings*, opera.

PITTMAN, EVELYN. *Oklahoma is My Home*, for SATB chorus.

PRICE, FLORENCE B. *Cobbler* (words by David Morton), for voice and piano.

————. *Colonial Dance Symphony*, for orchestra.

————. *Concert Overture No. 1* (based on Negro spirituals), for orchestra.

————. *Concert Overture No. 2* (based on three Negro spirituals), for orchestra.

———. *Concerto in D*, for violin and orchestra.

———. *The Dawn is Awake*, for voice and piano.

———. *The Dream Ship*, for voice and piano.

———. *Fantasy in Purple* (words by Langston Hughes), for voice and piano.

———. *God Gives Me You* (words by Nora Connally), for voice and piano; SATB chorus and piano.

———. *Lincoln Walks at Midnight*, for SATB chorus and orchestra.

———. *Mississippi River Symphony*, for orchestra.

———. *Moods*, for flute, clarinet, and piano.

———. *Negro Folksongs in Counterpoint*, for string quartet.

———. *The Oak*, tone poem for orchestra.

———. *Organ Sonata No. 1*.

———. *Passacaglia and Fugue*, for organ.

———. *Quintet for Piano and Strings*.

———. *Rhapsody for Piano and Orchestra*.

———. *Sea Gulls*, for SSA chorus and string orchestra.

———. *Song of Hope* (words by composer), for voice and orchestra.

———. *Songs of the Oak*, tone poem for orchestra.

———. *Song of the Open Road*, for voice and piano.

———. *Spring Journey*, for SSA chorus and string orchestra.

———. *Suite for Brasses and Piano*.

———. *Suite of Dances for Orchestra*.

———. *Suite for Organ*.

———. *Symphony in d minor*, for orchestra.

———. *Symphony in g minor*, for orchestra.

———. *To My Little Son* (words by Julia Johnson Davis), for voice and piano.

———. *Travel's End* (words by Mary Falwell Hoisington), for voice and piano.

———. *Variations on a Folksong*, for organ.

———. *The Waves of Breffney*, for SATB chorus a cappella.

———. *The Wind and the Sea*, for mixed chorus and string orchestra.

———. *Winter Idyl* (words by David Morton), for voice and piano.

Discography

BONDS, MARGARET. *He's Got the Whole World in His Hands; Sit Down Servant.* Performed by Leontyne Price. Orchestra directed by Leonard De Paur on *Swing Low Sweet Chariot.* Fourteen spirituals. RCA - LSC 2600.

———. *I Wish I Knew How it Would Feel to be Free; Sinner Please Don't Let This Harvest Pass; Standin' in the Need of Prayer.* Performed by Leontyne Price and the Rust College Choir directed by Lassaye Van Buren Holmes. RCA - LSC 3183.

PERRY, JULIA. *Homunculus C. F.* for percussion, harp, and piano, performed by the Manhattan Percussion Ensemble, conducted by Paul Price. Composers Recordings, Inc. CRI-S252.

———. *A Short Piece for Orchestra.* Performed by the Imperial Philharmonic Orchestra of Tokyo, conducted by William Strickland. Composers Recordings, Inc. CRI-145.

———. *Stabat Mater.* For contralto and string quartet or string orchestra. Performed by Makiko Asakura, mezzo-soprano; the Japan Philharmonic Symphony Orchestra, conducted by William Strickland. Composers Recordings, Inc. CRI-133.

PRICE, FLORENCE. *My Soul's Been Anchored in de Lord.* Performed by Marian Anderson. Victor 1799 (out of print).

———. Performed by Ellabelle Davis. London LPS-182 (out of print).

———. Performed by Leontyne Price. Orchestra conducted by Leonard De Paur on *Swing Low Sweet Chariot.* Fourteen spirituals RCA - LSC 2600.

Index